Sauntering Thru

Lessons in Ambition, Minimalism, and Love on the Appalachian Trail

By

Cody James Howell, PhD

"Raiden"

CONTENTS

Copyright
Acknowledgement
Prologue
A Decades-Long Approach Trail 1
A Journey of Two-Thousand Miles Starts with... 8
To The Top of Georgia and New Beginnings 16
Nantahala Basecamp, Springtime Romance 24
My First Nights on the Appalachian Trail 31
Into The Smoky Mountains 36
Making the Best of It 45
Finding Community in the Wilderness 52
Virginia is for Lovers 62
Resolve, Dashed Against the Rocks 70
City Skylines and Rocky Escarpments 81
Fortitude Tested in the Swamps of Vermont 88
Whose Idea Was This Anyway? 97
Alpine Wonderland 102
The Halcyon Days of Maine 113
Epilogue: Post Trail, Marriage, and Our Next Adventure 126
Appendix A – Post Trail Mental Health in the Thru-hiking Community ... 132
Appendix B – Practical Lessons on Long Distance Sauntering ... 142
About The Author 185

Copyright © 2020 Cody James Howell PhD

All rights reserved

The characters and events portrayed in this book are described as accurately as possilble. Some names have been changed to protect privacy.

No part of this book may be reproduced, or stored in a retrieval system, or transmitted in any form or by any means, electronic, mechanical, photocopying, recording, or otherwise, without express written permission of the publisher.

Cover design by: Yarikart
Printed in the United States of America

ACKNOWLEDGEMENT

First and foremost, I would like to thank my parents for helping me get to the trail, helping us get back off it, and for all the assistance in between.

I also want to extend tremendous gratitude to all the trail angels that make thru-hiking possible and more enjoyable in so many ways. In particular, I want to extend appreciation to:

Longhorn

Camaro Pete

And

Harlem Valley Photography

Finally, a hiker needn't walk long on the Appalachian Trail to realize how many lives it touches and how much work is required to deliver that experience. A thru-hike depends not only on countless hiking clubs and committees across its length, but also on trail towns, hostels, and trail angels who provide their much needed services. To them all, thank you.

Dedication

To Debra (Chilly Bin), as a love letter and memoir of our relationship and the grand adventure that shaped it.

And to the thru-hiking community at large.

PROLOGUE

As I look about this small patch of woods in mid-Ohio, I realize it pales next to the seemingly endless wilderness I spent so many weeks traversing last year. The gentle hills with their small groves of oak and maple, pretty though they are, only make me long for the mountains once again. It was the journey of a lifetime, an arduous ordeal for mind and body alike; I wish now that it had never ended.

A year ago I finished hiking the Appalachian Trail (AT), a tremendously challenging endeavor, and I was forever changed. My world today is quite different than it was then – enduring life in a global pandemic, separated from my partner by visa and border restrictions, facing political unrest which tests the very foundations of democracy. It makes me wish I were back on that trail; all I want to do is get away from everything and hike.

Completing the AT is not a journey one makes casually: walking the whole trail took me more than four months. When I summited Mount Katahdin in Maine – a mountain I'd dreamed about for many years – I had walked 2192 miles and climbed a total elevation gain equivalent to summiting Mount Everest sixteen times. Triumphantly, I stood on that peak with my wife-to-be, "Chilly Bin" (her given trail name), who I had met on day two of the trail and with whom I had spent nearly every moment over the previous 143 days. Reaching this point was an unparalleled achievement, and at the same time it was really little more than another mountain on a trail full of them. I realized in a burst of emotional Technicolor the truth behind the age-old wisdom that the journey is more important than its destination.

To explain this feeling, and the adventure as a whole, I use the word 'Saunter' – the perfect word to explain what thru-hiking (walking a long trail end to end) entails. John Muir preferred that we saunter through mountains rather than hiking them, his distaste for this more common term is widely known among nature enthusiasts. But it was Henry David Thoreau who first described his spiritual relationship to the woods in terms of his "sauntering" through them. Contentious then as it is now, he gave the word two possible meanings: the first describes one who is without land, or home, and who is therefore free to be at home wherever they should find themselves, and the second, more commonly accepted, describes a person who undertakes a holy pilgrimage, often accepting alms or donations to sustain them on their journey. I find it charming that both definitions apply perfectly to the thru-hiker; and moreover, that the ambiguity of this word mirrors the nebulous nature of thru-hiking itself. Quite a romantic view of what is essentially voluntary homelessness, don't you think?

At its core, a thru-hike acts to destroy preconceived notions: who we are, what we want, our goals, plans, and beliefs about ourselves and about the world we live in. Even now, months after completing the AT, I continue to gain clarity on the meaning of my thru-hike. It was nothing like I could have expected and yet everything it was promised to be. People often ask if the purpose of a thru-hike is to 'find yourself' or to have 'a great time' or some other anodyne Hallmark-card version of the truth. Maybe for some this is an adequate description, but I tend to think in more brutal terms about what the AT can do to a person's psyche. Even so, I can't deny seeing the effects of my time spent as "Raiden", the AT thru-hiker, everywhere I look.

So many books about thru-hiking involve someone trying to escape something – a job, depression, or a feeling of being lost in the world, for example. This gives the impression that few actually do it as a positive challenge; however, this misrepresents the truth in my estimation.

To this point, David Miller (AWOL) said in his now famous

book, "Nothing is wrong with my life. My family is outstanding. I have what most people would consider to be a decent job. I'm not unhappy, and I'm not hiking to escape from anything. My life is precariously normal."

This last line hits the nail on the head: thru-hiking the AT is one of the least normal things many people will ever experience, and is perhaps the best way to break from our old habits and from modern society.

My own story is not so different. I have always been driven by my ambitions, seeking the greatest challenges I could find. This motivation was as much a factor in choosing to become a neuroscientist as it was to thru-hiking the Appalachian Trail; in fact, both stemmed from childhood dreams (more on that later). The possibility of **NOW** (read: spring 2019) being the right time fell into my lap like a gift from the heavens. As I neared the completion of my PhD, I gave it everything I had in order to finish in February, thereby allowing me time to reach Springer Mountain, the southern trail head, by April. I never had a single doubt that I could finish the trail, barring some unforeseen and critical injury. Nothing short of a broken leg would stop me from finishing, no matter the challenges ahead. Although fears of such dangers plagued the minds of my family, no one voiced any doubts that I would succeed.

I share with you my near overconfidence, and ability to achieve other difficult goals, as a means of providing contrast. Although I started the trail chasing an ambition as old as I can remember, I was humbled by the unrelenting physical and mental stress that is long-distance hiking. Thru-hiking has a way of wearing down the practiced persona of our cultural being, washing away the trappings of the modern world, and baring our true self for all to see.

This has the secondary benefit of increasing the speed at which relationships are both formed and destroyed. *Relationship time*, a form of temporal relativity that I've created for convenience, flows at light speed when the distractions of polite society are supplanted by weeklong hiker filth, poor nutrition, and worse weather. Did I mention mosquito swarms dense as fog on a fresh morning? Oh, and the added bonus of constant low-level sleep deprivation, which is what happens when you put a light sleeper such as myself on an inflatable mat that sounds like kids wrapped in aluminum foil jumping around in a pit of balloons. Enduring this 24/7 is the quickest way to understand that acceptance is a better path to finding peace than fighting the inevitable. Going through this with someone else is truly a test unlike any other; and in terms of intimate relationships, no one has patience or energy left over for dating etiquette.

Finally, my experience highlights the truth behind the oft-heard AT wisdom that 'the trail provides'. First, the trail provided me with time. This part is obvious. All you really have to do each day is walk; it's pretty simple on the face of it. However, having spent my whole life in education, and finishing my PhD in neuroscience just prior to starting my hike, I was constantly under pressure to stay focused and had experienced little time to think so broadly. Getting away from that and simplifying my life gave me the time to see a better path forward. Second, the trail provided me with my best friend and partner. I tell our story for her – as a love letter of sorts. I had recently gotten out of a relationship and told myself firmly that I would avoid entering another one for at least a little while.

That illusion lasted exactly one day on the trail and I couldn't be happier to have been so wrong.

Third, the trail provided, or forced, simple living; it acts as a medium for practicing mindfulness through the pursuit of minimalism. At first I thought this pursuit was leading me to ultralight backpacking, an approach which stresses counting ounces and pounds first and foremost. However, the real payoff came from a more nuanced approach, focusing instead on the mental state that results from decluttering one's life. Well, that and removing all the extra junk in my pack that kept poking me in the back. This extreme minimalism and simplicity, a core feature of the thru-hiking experience, has strengthened my connection to the outdoors and has bettered nearly every other aspect of my life in one way or anther.

I want to help the reader understand what thru-hiking is, and perhaps more importantly, what it isn't. I also hope to provide a better understanding to those who support, or put up with, thru-hikers: the families, friends, trail angels, and dreamers who think about the trail and the people who hike it. It's also a chance to treat yourself, at my expense, to the mental lows of walking miles over ankle-breaking rocks while being swarmed with endless biting insects; and narrowly escaping numerous adventure-ending pitfalls such as dangerous hitchhikes, nearly shattering kneecaps, and barely avoiding hypothermia, twice.

These low points anchored this grand adventure. It was the perfect experience; and I got to share it with my best friend, whom I met against all expectations, while out in the woods covered in dirt. This story acts as a real-life account of the beauty and difficulty of thru-hiking, while also providing a few insights on minimalism and the other lessons taught by a summer living the simple life.

Children love imagination, the possibility of stepping through portals to a different reality. As adults, this skill is often worn down with the passing of time. This book, and more so the adventure within, is a chance to recapture our former wanderlust and imaginative vision of reality. This is what I seek to offer the reader, because that is what the trail has offered to me.

At the very least, perhaps you can imagine walking along with Chilly and me on our journey to Mount Katahdin.

A DECADES-LONG APPROACH TRAIL

"Anywhere is within walking distance, if you've got the time." –Stephen Wright

"This trail goes all the way to Maine!"

This was my first memory of the Appalachian Trail, seared into my ten-year-old mind, awestruck by the audacity of such an impossible task upon discovering the worn, brown trail marker at Newfound Gap in Tennessee.

How one approaches the concept of starting a thru-hike is almost certainly as diverse as the people who hit the trail. My own journey began two decades before I set foot on Springer Mountain, during one of our many family trips to the Great Smoky Mountains National Park. At a young and impressionable age, I stepped out of the family van at Newfound Gap, the lowest drivable pass in the park, and wandered over to the Rockefeller Monument from which Franklin Delano Roosevelt dedicated the Great Smoky Mountains National Park for the "permanent enjoyment of the people". Just around the corner from this site is a rather unassuming trailhead and an old mile marker which, unbeknownst to me at the time, would become the site of many great memories throughout the coming years.

The sign reads, among other less interesting things: "Katahdin Maine – 1972.0 miles".

I can remember thinking with an astonishment that pervades my mind even now, "How could anyone be expected to do that!?"

That was the first year I stepped foot on the Appalachian Trail. Though we would only walk a mile or two then, a seed was planted in my mind that would be tended and nourished every time I set foot on a trail from then on.

Prior to thru-hiking the Appalachian Trail, education was all I knew. I would end up spending the entirety of my adult life to that point, in stuffy classrooms, and later, state of the art research facilities. Although I had done countless day-hikes and car camping trips prior to college, once I left my small town and headed to the city I remained considerably more removed from nature for the next several years. During four years of my undergraduate education, and the first three years in graduate school, I would remain with my nose in the books, removed from more natural environments.

It took a bit of friendly cajoling from a fellow grad student to make me remember what I had been missing.

"So do you like backpacking? Are there any good trails around here?" I was asked one day after getting to know Andy as an outdoorsman and adventurer. I loved to hike so I told him sure, I loved it; but it had been a while.

"Awesome, we should go soon!"

And so I would pack what little gear I had at the time into a duffel bag and jump in my car to meet him and his girlfriend at the local park.

As you can probably tell, I was ill prepared for what he had planned. I showed up with a ten pound Coleman tent in its duffle bag carrier and little to no idea that he planned to hike first then camp, not the other way around. Needless to say, I was the target of all the jokes that trip.

On the upside, I was immediately taken to an outdoors shop and picked up my first piece of actual backpacking gear: a 30 liter internal frame Marmot backpack. Small for overnight trips, but plenty of strapping on the outside for extra gear.

That trip we settled for pitching the Coleman on a little hill just a short walk from the cars and enjoying some time in the woods; but the pack I got, and the education from a simple night out of my comfort zone, was just the sort of kick in the pants I needed.

• • •

Over the next three years, I continued working long hours on my experiments; but, I would take every opportunity I could (actually very few, and all too short) to get out in the woods. I had experiments that would take many days or weeks of continuous effort, with only a small break now and then when I could step away. Of course, my advisor expected me to perform some other work during that time, like writing my thesis. I was reprimanded more than once for taking a weekend off despite having worked every single day for months on end.

Work life balance? Nothing more than a fleeting ideal for me.

So I took to 'writing' with a voice recorder, or voice to text programs, so I could work on my thesis while I walked. I learned to hike faster so I could do and see more in what little time I had away from the lab bench.

Although I continued to go with friends once in a while, I went by myself more and more over time. I found that I wanted to go farther, and do harder trails, than those who got me into the hobby. Somewhere below the level of conscious thought existed a pressing motivation to view every hike as an experiment; testing gear, strength, endurance, and myself in attempt to get better at backpacking (whatever that means).

Maybe you would have urged me to relax a little, to slow down and enjoy those trips rather than seeing them as a means to an end. I couldn't help myself, it was a calling, a relentless gnawing that took hold of me; once I truly grasped the meaning of backpacking and saw that my childhood dream was possible, I knew I had to pursue it to the logical extreme.

What is the pinnacle of backpacking? How can one determine a "pro" from an amateur in our "sport"? Can't say I ever really had an answer to what it means to "be good at backpacking", but maybe the answer was somewhere over that next mountain.

• • •

My passion for backpacking, and my calling to become a thru-hiker, was preceded only by similar drives to pursue science. And much like backpacking, my initial expectations for what science is and how one actually performs it were somewhat removed from reality.

My first memory of science, as a kid, came from watching Jurassic Park. While others were fascinated by the dinosaurs themselves, my interests laid more squarely on the paleontologists and geneticists (the dinosaurs were pretty cool too, obviously).

My interest in science blossomed greatly through my young adulthood, shaped even more by my readings in fiction than from the textbooks. I was always more attracted by the possibilities than by what had already been done. By the end of high school, I had settled on biomedical engineering; and while not science per se, it did get me more exposure to biology where I would eventually find my passion. I left engineering after only one semester, spending the rest of my undergraduate career in every field I could find associated with the human brain.

I mentioned before that science, in practice, is not necessarily what it seemed from afar. As a graduate student, I was expected to dedicate nothing short of my entire life to the lab bench for the next five to seven years. Much like thru-hiking, science has some rather extreme ups and downs; and much like hiking for half a year non-stop to then summit a mountain which you have dreamed about since your childhood, making an important scientific discovery requires a ceaseless grind toward the summit.

The result is knowing something that only you have known in the entire history of humanity – at least for that single moment before you shout it from the rooftops. There are certain feelings in life, like these, which can only be known after long, hard climbs up steep and treacherous mountains.

That being said, science is really just putting one foot in front of the other, endlessly; or, at risk of muddling my metaphor, repetitively moving liquids from this vial to that, and running behavioral or surgical algorithms over and over and over. Those glorious summits from which you view eternity and feel like the tallest person on earth are few and far between.

I give you this small piece of background about myself to show you that while I may have been short on physical preparation, I went as deep as I could on mental preparation by submitting myself to such grueling intellectual challenges. Even though I didn't realize at the time, my education would have a tremendous impact on how I would perceive, and tolerate, the challenges of my next adventure.

●●●

In late 2018, my two childhood passions were coming together in a yin and yang balance between harmony and dissonance, pulling me this way and that. I had progressively hiked harder and harder trails, and dialed in my backpacking gear a little more each time. In the last year before I graduated, I became quite serious and specific about designing a kit capable of completing a thru-hike of the AT. The only problem was, I still didn't know if getting away from science long enough would be possible.

At the same time, I was constantly under pressure to decide a career path. On one hand, the standard path of an academic scientist would require bone grinding amounts of time-dependent effort over the next four years with no down-time between grad school and a postdoctoral research position. On the other hand,

I was considering a non-traditional route as a research analyst in the investment banking world of Wall Street. The first path would keep me at the lab bench for countless years to come, with the end goal of furthering our understanding in a relatively specific and small way. The latter option, which I settled on at nearly the final possible moment, would allow, in my estimation, the ability to leave science in the short term and return to it later with more political and economic influence, not to mention more personal freedom.

Because it took me so long to settle on a non-traditional career for a scientist, I had also put off any real planning on the thru-hike until January 2019. I began to realize that I could form a gap long enough to thru-hike, then come back and apply with yet another unique experience on my resume.

The plan became real before my eyes, a much needed oasis in the desert first seen as just another illusion. At once I could feel it almost tangibly in my fingers, and I set to work getting in shape for the trail. My friend Nish talked me into a gym membership, and lent me his weight vest to train. Over the next month, I set to work on the Stairmaster and incline treadmill in between yoga classes designed to increase my flexibility. Of course, let's not forget that I was writing my thesis and preparing a defense in front of my entire department at the same time. I was still using the miracle that is voice recording to write both my thesis and my presentation while training in the gym – and hiking if I could get away.

It may interest you to know that I'm writing this book using the same technique. Don't fix what isn't broke!

●●●

I want to impress on you here the degree to which my life was firmly rooted in themes of ambition and multitasking. That lifestyle is everything they say it is, both rewarding and stressful to the point of being unhealthy. More than once during my graduate career I dealt with health problems related to physical and mental stress, including both ulcers and hernias; the latter of which resulted from going too hard with too much weight while backpacking in the wee hours between experiments.

Partially as a result of this stressful lifestyle, I discovered the benefit of practicing Buddhist meditative techniques. I like to think of these techniques as a way to declutter the mental landscape, and refocus my mind on the important things. Little more, little less. I would find these techniques quite useful in the months to come.

It was with this balance between stressed and overworked, and the desire to seek simplicity, with which my long approach trail finally led to the base of Springer Mountain and the start of the AT. I finished my PhD, had my post trail career goals laid out and crystallized, and I had set for myself the goal of thru-hiking the Appalachian Trail first and foremost as a meditative and contemplative experience that would deliver me back to some semblance of simple living.

Oddly enough, the act of seeking simplicity is itself a goal, an ambition, and a preconceived notion of what thru-hiking is and what it might deliver. The irony that I would soon come to realize is the trail doesn't care about your goals. The more you try to define a thru-hike, the more your experience will thrash against your expectations. The trail is nothing if not a destroyer of preconceptions. Little did I know that the ambition and drive with which I set out on the trail would be wholly subverted and transformed into something completely unpredictable. I was blindsided, all my plans for this hike went straight out the window (or over the cliff as it were). Almost everything would change for me on this adventure, my career plans and my family plans alike.

They say a thru-hike will change your life. I can't say I wasn't warned.

A JOURNEY OF TWO-THOUSAND MILES STARTS WITH...

"I went to the woods because I wished to live deliberately, to front only the essential facts of life, and see if I could not learn what it had to teach, and not, when I came to die, discover that I had not lived." –Henry David Thoreau

On April 4th, 2019 I woke up in a hotel room only a few miles from Springer Mountain. I could see it off in the distance, cloaked in a blue haze like some Bob Ross painting, as my parents and I packed up the car. We drove out early in the morning and reached the Amicalola Falls visitor center.

I checked-in and received my thru-hiker number for the year: #1854. Starting pack weight: 23 pounds, including food and water.

After sitting through a short briefing on how to thru-hike, I began this glorious undertaking with a grueling climb up the 600-odd stairs winding back and forth in front of the waterfall that acts as a gateway to the grandfather of American long trails.

It was eight miles to the official start of the Appalachian Trail and the peak of Springer Mountain. A sign at the beginning of the approach trail warned hikers it may take more than six hours to get there.

"I'm not sure who counted," I said out loud as I'm prone to do while alone in the woods, "mom and dad will be there in two, so that better be wrong".

Springer Mountain is rather unassuming among the other low-lying mountains in the area. I wasn't quite sure I had made it there until I started hearing voices at the summit. Then, suddenly, there was no question I had arrived. My parents had just reached the summit themselves, almost two hours on the nose!

A small plaque marks the site, and a hiker journal serving as a register is hidden in the stone beside it. Both are quite easy to miss, I'm sure a substantial number of thru-hikers simply walk on by.

My parents and I had lunch at the top, then made our way a couple of miles down Springer together before they bid me farewell on my adventure. It was a good day for hiking – we had waited several days for a break in the rain before heading to Georgia from our family home in mid-Ohio. This day blessed us with a temporary lull in the storms, providing me with a full day of hiking in clear weather before the rains started anew.

The white blazes, painted six inches tall by two inches wide, seemed to increase in frequency after finishing the approach trail. Now, and for most of the trail going north, we would be guided through the woods by these blazes posted with the frequency of street lamps along the sidewalk. You can't easily go astray.

That evening I made my way into Stover Creek Shelter, the second official shelter on the AT. My first day I walked a total of 11 miles, only three of which were on the AT proper. I shared the shelter that night with four others and a service dog. By the time I had reached camp, the fire was started and around it stood three figures sharing stories. I joined them and before long we were practicing our bear hangs in a nearby tree, trying not to get hit with the swinging bag of rocks which would allow us to suspend our food away from the reach of the black bears which were notorious in this part of the country.

Around dusk, our fourth companion stumbled down the trail

with his trusty dog and gigantic pack which he would later tell us weighed 50 pounds and had more than he could ever need. After hearing his pots and pans clink and clank down the trail for ten minutes before we even saw him, I needed little convincing he was over packed.

Luckily, the rain held off until we were all inside; but then it poured down all night. This would be one of only four times that I stayed in a shelter on the AT, the noise and odor of these places where hikers gather at night quickly wore on my patience. I have enough trouble sleeping as it is.

The second morning, and my first waking up on trail, was bright and warm after the heavy rains of the previous evening. I boiled my tea and had breakfast with the group. It must have been about nine o'clock by the time I hit the privy, a standard fixture at shelters on the AT. Little more than a shed with a platform and plastic throne, these privies work using a simplified composting system that requires a handful of duff or pine chips after each use.

Upon hearing footsteps approaching, I called out "just a minute!" as I finished pulling up my onesie.

Oh right, it's worth mentioning that I started the trail with a Merino wool onesie as a base layer. Very comfortable, no rubbing and chafing around the midline like you might have with pants. This particular onesie was bright purple and made me stand out like a sore thumb. I was clearly the most "fashionable" member of our hiker trash (a self-referential term used by thru-hikers) gathering that morning. But I would get rid of the onesie soon enough – too much of a pain to it get on and off. Fashion sense had nothing to do with that decision because; as you will continue to learn, I have none.

Anyway, I left the privy and quickly brushed past a female figure without recognizing it was someone altogether new. To be honest, I was still a bit shy about using a shared toilet in front of strangers of the opposite sex, so I had my head lowered in irrational embarrassment. Luckily, such ideals of modesty from the modern western world would quickly be dashed to bits against the primitive natural demands of thru-hiking. A few moments later this newcomer would meet us at the shelter. An early riser, she had already walked from the previous shelter near Springer Mountain. She said her name was 'Chilly Bin', and her accent suggested she had traveled far to thru-hike the AT.

• • •

Chilly Bin left first, she was only passing through after all. The rest of us trickled out one by one after we finished breakfast. Before long, I met up with Marvel, who I had met the previous evening, and walked with her for a bit talking about our lives prior to starting the trail; she shared an interesting story about doing some teaching in Japan. After a while we split up and I eventually found Shark Chow, a middle aged journalist and fellow shelter dweller from the night before. We stumbled upon our first "trail magic" set up on a small side road where it crossed the trail. Chilly Bin was already there, warming her feet near a propane heater.

Trail magic, another name for the charity given to thru-hikers by people we call "Trail Angels", is always a welcome sight on a long hike. This one involved grilled hot dogs along with an array of chips, cookies, and ice-cold soft drinks in coolers. On that note, I will point out that 'chilly bin' is the name for a cooler in New Zealand, and Chilly's excitement upon seeing such trail magic is how she earned her name on a previous long trail. Trail names such as this are a time honored tradition of thru-hiking life; almost no one uses their real name on long distance trails, at least not the whole way. Bestowed upon you by another hiker, trail names are generally related to something unique that you have done or said; and, it's usually frowned upon to name yourself – better to let the trail provide.

After eating a few snacks and talking with the trail angels a bit,

I headed back to the trail on my own. Not a mile away from the trail magic I ran into Tavner again, another one of my new shelter friends, who had skipped the trail magic not knowing what it was. Soon Chilly caught up and we all walked to Gooch Mountain Shelter together.

To my surprise, there were roughly 40 other thru-hikers at the shelter by the time we arrived, and a ridge runner helped organize the tent pads. These pads were little more than flat, packed dirt. Simple as it comes, two to a space. He asked Chilly and I if we were together. We looked at each other and shrugged, so he stuck us together.

I could tell immediately Chilly was not your average hiker after she whipped off her shirt, stood there with just a bra and shorts, and checked her new tattoo for potential damage. By the time I noticed all of this happening in plain view, she was rubbing a balm onto that tattoo with the nonchalant attitude of a small child picking his nose on the subway.

Slightly taken aback, I said, "I can walk away and give you some privacy if you want".

"Yeh, nah. This is normal," her Kiwi expression almost mocking my naïveté about trail culture.

And it IS normal. I just hadn't been ready for it. I hadn't yet settled into the norms of thru-hiking. Polite society was left in the city, and the rugged trail would teach us all to stop sweating the small stuff – like getting half naked, or completely naked in some cases, in front of strangers.

But this wasn't Chilly Bin's first rodeo. I would learn, over time, that Chilly Bin's experience leading up to the Appalachian Trail was extensive, and this experience would show itself in everything from her gear choices to the topics of our conversations. She wore sandals, and carried a pack smaller than my own; and she had traveled halfway around the world, by herself, just to walk the AT. Prior to this thru-hike attempt, she had hiked almost the entire Pacific Crest Trail and completed a full section-hike of (the) Te Araroa in her native New Zealand. She had also spent just as much time backpacking through Southeast Asia.

Needless to say, any backpacker would benefit from her experience.

I spent the rest that evening floating around chatting with various other strangers at the shelter: a college aged rock climber attempting a thru-hike with her mom, a stoner who was very interested in finding some psychedelic mushrooms, and a writer walking long trails all over the country along with his dog. I never saw any of them again after that, but that was the case with most people I meet while thru-hiking.

"Single serving friends" as Tyler Durden would have said in Fight Club. Sometimes these are the best kind – you only have time to see their good side.

● ● ●

The next morning, I had barely rolled out of bed (a sleeping pad and mummy bag, such as it was) before noticing that Chilly had already broken camp. She would head off before I even finished breakfast.

On my way out of camp, Tavner called out to me – he said he had thought of a perfect trail name for me overnight. I had several pieces of unique gear which, I thought correctly, might influence my trail name. It turned out the conical hat that I bought from China would inspire my name: Raiden. Tavner pointed out that it shared a likeness with the Mortal Kombat character by the same name; my character of choice, just by chance.

I gladly accepted, and made my way back to the trail.

By lunch time, I approached another shelter that was located just a quarter-mile down a blue-blazed side trail, so I made my way there expecting to have a nice place to sit while I ate. By chance, or simply as a result of timing, Chilly was already starting her own lunch in the very same shelter. And so it went for the first week on the trail: she would rise early in the morning and head out alone and I, walking at a faster pace than her, eventually caught up around lunch time. As far as I know, this was not planned by either of us. Most of those days we would spend the afternoon walking together and talking about everything and anything you could imagine. You get to know a person pretty quick when you spend most of the day with little to do.

This day after Gooch Mountain Shelter, we were slated to climb up Blood Mountain, then drop down into Neels Gap for our first restock of the trail. Blood Mountain was the climb rumored to cause so many thru-hiker hopefuls to quit at Neels Gap, subsequently throwing their shoes into the notorious tree at the bottom of the mountain. However, we climbed it having a full conversation, and upon reaching the top, wondered what all the fuss was about.

We took a few photos with the ancient shelter, mostly unused in recent years due to all the bear activity. The view from Blood Mountain can be enjoyed from a rock slab adjacent to the old shelter where we relaxed on the mountainside, snacking and enjoying the well-earned vista.

Later that day we would descend into Neels Gap. A gorgeous stone structure known as Mountain Crossings awaited, along with its overpriced trail food and free pack shakedowns where the overburdened hiker might be excited to drop a few pounds. However, I quickly found that most people, including myself, were primarily excited about the frozen pizzas.

A large group of us sat at the picnic tables eating our first "quality" food in days, sharing our excitement about the new adventure, and charging our phones in an outlet that was placed precariously close to a spigot where we could refill our water bottles. I also discovered a new norm at Neels Gap which I would eventually come to tolerate but never fully accept. That is, being forced to leave our packs outside of shops, unguarded, and in the public eye for anyone to... admire.

The only major change I made at Mountain Crossings was to start rocking a fanny pack. Yes, it looks as ridiculous as you likely imagine.

Chilly had spent the previous day talking about the advantages of fanny packs: storing your snacks, keeping your phone handy, taking a little weight from the pack and redistributing it to your center of balance. I was sold, but I also overpaid for my first one. Like everything else at Mountain Crossings, that fanny pack cost twice as much and had half the quality of what I really wanted; and I would end up replacing it with a cheaper, waterproof version soon enough.

Our restock frequency more or less followed this pattern the entire trail: three to five days of hiking, then a restock. We planned to never carry more than six to eight pounds of food at a time. This led to a critical realization about the trail; it could be perceived not as one long multi-month hike, but rather as a consecutive series of multi-day sections.

Town hopping, as we called it.

In this way, the monumental task of thru-hiking was broken down into more manageable, bit-sized sections that eased the mental burden of such an endeavor.

TO THE TOP OF GEORGIA AND NEW BEGINNINGS

> *"We must be willing to get rid of the life we've planned, so as to have the life that is waiting for us. The old skin has to be shed before the new one can come."* —Joseph Campbell

Neels Gap is one of the great filters on the Appalachian Trail, a place where many hikers give up after being faced with a greater challenge than they were prepared to accept. For those who continue onward, two groups seemed to form: those who had struggled to get here and were ready for a shower and soft bed (both of which were provided for a fee), and those who found themselves well prepared for the trials of Southern Georgia and were still feeling fresh. A group of us, a primarily younger crowd including myself, fell into this latter category.

Most of us planned to stay the night just a little way up the mountain from Neels Gap, and trickled out in ones and twos after dinner. I walked with a thru-hiker from Pennsylvania who went by Gypsy at the time, and later by Driftwood. Trail names are a fluid concept.

We discussed things we had left behind to walk the trail; that I had just finished my PhD, while she was on a sabbatical from the bakery she had started with her sister. In these early days, many of us were quite excited to have some time away from whatever we had left behind. Too early to miss home, the excitement was still raw and invigorating.

Upon reaching the campsite that evening, we were greeted with a smiling face that I would see frequently through the hike. John, as he introduced himself, also switched names a few times before eventually settling on Survivor. But he was always John to us. He joined Driftwood and me where we had positioned ourselves away from the larger group. We were just finishing our camp setup when Chilly and Red came up the hill to join us. The five of us sat and discussed gear that evening, and it quickly became clear that Chilly was the most experienced in our group.

That evening, John was reprimanded by the group for dropping crumbs near our tent site, and I got schooled in Dyneema fabric (the lightest weight fabric used in the top-of-the-line tents) after mistakenly wondering if my own tent was made of that or silnylon (silicone impregnated nylon). All in good fun of course, we weren't actually hard on each other for the understandable ignorance of people in a completely new experience. John had never been on a multi-day backpacking trip before, and I had trained and studied backpacking mostly on my own without ever purchasing the high-end gear.

Chilly and Red, on the other hand, had their kits even more dialed in that I did. Despite my own training, I still had much to learn from others. And even with the wide range of experience in our group, we all had plenty to share and thoroughly enjoyed the new company.

Experiences like that evening are particularly interesting because it goes to show that thru-hikers, and all hikers to some extent, share a kinship and common purpose that make for easy bonds whether long and short. There are countless instances like this one that I remember from the trail, memories tied to faces and sometimes names, but rarely to contact information. If I learned two things from this type of interaction it would be to take pictures of the people I meet and not just the sights I see, and to exchange contact information for keeping in contact after the trail. It's easy to begin seeing your fellow thru-hikers as family, and being able to contact them later is worth more than one could ever imagine.

The next morning, we were headed to the campsite at the summit of Blue Mountain. It absolutely poured down rain that day, and to keep warm, Red and I decided to race up the mountain. Red, a kid freshly out of high school taking full advantage of his summer before starting college, was taller than me by a foot, all of it in his legs. Rarely had I been so thoroughly eclipsed by a hiker's uphill speed. Unfortunately for Red, this would soon show its downside in the form of knee pain severe enough to split us up.

There were two ways to head into Hiawassee, before or after Blue Mountain. Red took the first exit so that he could rest his knee ASAP, while Chilly and I headed up to the campsite.

In this short stretch of trail, I had the opportunity to learn more about Chilly without others around. She was trained as an engineer, but only worked as much as necessary in order to hike each summer.

"It's not that I dislike work, it's just that I like tramping more!"

I made a note to myself: tramping = hiking in Kiwi terminology.

I had a bit of a laugh and told her what a tramp was in the States. She didn't find that nearly as comical as I did.

Blue Mountain Shelter sits on the summit in a lovely location flat enough for 20 or 30 tents and an expansive view to the north overlooking the valley on the way to Hiawassee. Chilly and I pitched our tents away from the larger groups but ended up socialized with many of them. There were two larger groups of people we met here which would be in our bubble throughout the trail. The first was a family of five, the Corey family, whose children ranged between seven and thirteen. Though we didn't talk with the Corey's as much on Blue Mountain, we would spend multiple days hiking with or around them in the near future.

The other group was a "tramily", or trail family, a group of unrelated hikers who formed tight bonds and attempted to complete the whole trail together. For dinner, we all sat in a circle telling stories, talking about our trail food preferences, and watching a rather comical pair of guys climbing this skinny little tree in a futile attempt to retrieve their bear bag which had gotten stuck.

It's worth pointing out that this took place only five days from the start of the trail, so I was somewhat skeptical of the likelihood that a tramily could form such close bonds so quickly or that all of them would finish the trail given only an average 20-25% success rate for thru-hiking the AT.

Chilly echoed my skepticism, and recounted her experience in a tramily on the PCT which both failed to stick together and failed, almost to the person, to complete the trail. Of course, the unspoken implication of our conversation was that she and I would also be a temporary friendship – if the statistics could be believed.

I was wrong on across the board.

●●●

The next day turned into quite an adventure. The morning began with our first meeting of Dundee and Sandpig, two middle-aged gentlemen that we would run into countless times along the trail. Sandpig, so named due to being a cop from the Arizona desert, and Dundee who wore a distinctive hat reminiscent of his namesake. These cheery chaps would call us "The Kiwis" for some time, regardless of the fact that I was clearly not from New Zealand! Nevertheless, these two were having the time of their lives and I can't say I ever saw them unhappy on the trail. It was a pleasure to hike around them.

A few miles later we came to the road into Hiawassee, but instead of heading straight into town, we had planned to stay at "The Top of Georgia" Hostel located about a half mile down the road. We had been on the trail just under a week now and were beginning to feel like a shower was in order. Chilly's sandal-clad feet were caked in days of mud and grime, and my synthetic clothing smelled something like the dirty locker room of teenage boys. It was time for our first pit stop on the trail.

The hostel was an interesting place, and I say WAS because they have since closed their doors due to some controversy with the owner. They provided a free shuttle down to Hiawassee several times a day. During the ride, the owner talked *at* us the entire way about his backpacking experience and how to have a successful thru-hike. Apparently, this was one source of the controversy – I don't know all the details. It was a bit overbearing; but who cares, we were headed to town for the first time in what seemed like forever.

We had a good time in Hiawassee. The hostel had provided us with loner clothes while ours were in the wash. Hideous blue scrubs. Everyone around town knew exactly where we were staying that night.

This trail town, like nearly every other in the south, was a charming and welcoming retreat from the unforgiving wilderness from whence we came. If you have read "A Walk in the Woods" by Bill Bryson, you may be surprised to read such a kindly interpretation of these small, close-knit southern towns; but I feel it worth pointing out that not a single cyclops was spotted pumping gas, nor did we ever fear the Chainsaw Massacre just around the next corner. Sometimes banjo music is just a call to come and sit a spell, rather than the background music to a horror film!

We did our shopping before heading to the local Mexican restaurant. This place was all the rage within the community. Chilly and I were joined by Red, Tree Trunks (an Australian man experienced in iron-man and triathlons races), and Montana Jesus (named as such, I assume, due to the resemblance). Great food and even better company!

It's worth mentioning here that almost every thru-hiker we

spent much time with actually finished the trail, which is truly incredible given that 75 to 80% of those who start don't finish. It was also the case that most of the people I mentioned, including the two in the above paragraph, were semi-frequent fixtures all along the trail. This is what is referred to as a hiker "bubble", a cluster of hikers that move through the trail in a more or less cohesive fashion. Hiking around, but not with, each other.

Instead of catching the shuttle back to the hostel, we were instead approached by what would become the most familiar short yellow bus in my life. It pulled up beside us and the driver shouted out the door, "Who wants free candy!"

If you've spent any time in the thru-hiking community, you will surely recognize this to be Odie, the friendly hiker bum and organizer of the Hiker Yearbook. How lucky were we that he would be following the main NOBO thru-hiker bubble and found us just when we needed a ride. His bus is outfitted with a bed and couch, along with all the standard hippie décor.

But those offers of free candy? Always a deception after all...

● ● ●

The day before arriving at The Top of Georgia, I was beginning to experience knee pain of my own. Ankle pain too.

The knee pain was no surprise, I had an old ACL injury from pole-vaulting in high school that sometimes bothered me on the downhills. This despite the surgical repairs. Hiking everyday was only making it worse.

The ankle pain, on the other hand, was strange. I don't get rolled ankles you see, chalk that up to stretchy ligaments I guess. No this was something else. Luckily, Chilly had some codeine tablets she carried hiking (apparently that's easier to get in New Zealand), and I had one of those to help me get out of the woods.

I was also lucky to find a knee brace in the hiker box at The

Top of Georgia. These hiker boxes are like little treasure chests placed in various stores, churches, and hostels across the length of the AT. They provide a place where gear can be exchanged between thru-hikers at no cost. Driftwood had just tossed her knee brace in there, along with some KT tape, and I tried them both over the next week.

I later found that it was my shoes causing the problem. The Altra Lone Peak 4s I had trained in for months before the trail were spent. As soon as I picked up new shoes (the Altra Timp 1.5), I was back in business.

• • •

The morning after our visit to Hiawassee, Chilly and I woke before the sun, quietly gathered our things, and exited the bunk room into the brisk, calm dawn. Without a word to one another, we set off towards the trail. As the name "The Top of Georgia" would imply, today is the day we would cross our first state border.

Such border crossings are one of the measuring sticks of success during a thru-hike. We would be marking such progress 13 times as we walked through 14 states, and we approached the first with the excitement of recently adopted puppies. When we got there, another group was already taking pictures with the sign that said "N.C.".

We took our obligatory pictures and headed on our way. This location is not particularly picturesque, just a small saddle between mountains really. But now we were on our way to one of the most memorable mountain peaks of the entire trail (for us): Standing Indian.

We planned to camp at the summit, making it in time for the sunset and hoping we could get there early enough to have it all to ourselves. We succeeded, and were alone until the sky started turning shades of orange and purple. Just then, another couple came to join us, took a few pictures, and were on their way.

We pitched our tents around the fire ring, then sat propped up against a fallen log. By this point, we had only spent about nine days together; however, time on the trail passed slowly, every minute felt packed with novelty, and all we did was walk and talk. We had discussed everything from our past experiences and professions to goals both financial and familial. I was starting to think we were a pretty good match.

This all happened quite fast, but even so it felt right; it felt like our time together moved faster, and with more purpose, than it would have in any other scenario.

In my stumbling, school-boy approach I told her that I wanted more than just a hiking partner, that we had so much in common even though we grew up half the world apart, and that I thought we could do very well in a relationship. Luckily the sun had set enough by then that she couldn't see the redness in my face, or maybe she thought it was the cold rather than embarrassment; at least that's what I hoped as the blood filled my cheeks.

After a moment's hesitation, likely taken by surprise that I spared no time waiting, she agreed. And then I kissed her. We spent the rest of that evening enjoying the end of a spectacular day on a gorgeous mountain.

It was the beginning of something great.

NANTAHALA BASECAMP, SPRINGTIME ROMANCE

> *"Don't go into thru-hiking with an expectation of a result. The whole beauty of thru-hiking is learning how to give up control. So many things could go wrong – you have to let go of what the situation could be or should be and accept what is."* –Adrian "Felix Felicis" Harrison

We spent the morning after Standing Indian heading south by the compass, though we continued northward on the trail itself. How ridiculous, we thought, to loop down south just to head right back north! We could have cut nearly ten miles off the trip by simply continuing toward Tennessee.

The purpose of this "detour" was to climb over Albert Mountain. As we stood at its base, staring up at a near vertical rock face, we were clearly in for our hardest climb yet. Although only about 1000 vertical feet over two miles, the first half of that involves hands over head climbing before relaxing into a smooth stroll to the summit. For their effort, hikers are granted the option to climb a fire tower and take in the view from above the tree line; of course, one needs the willingness to climb several flights of stairs first. We dropped our packs at the base of the tower and continued our ascent. Once at the top we were greeted by a 360° view of the surrounding area, and we could pick out Standing Indian when we looked to the southwest. It's always satisfying to look back to places you had been hours, or even days, before. Looking to the north we saw rolling green hills and valleys, but couldn't yet recognize where we were meant to be heading. No matter, we would be there soon enough if we just follow the blazes.

After retrieving our packs at the base of the tower, we headed down from the summit where we came almost immediately to our first hiker-made mile marker.

"100", written in block letters made from sticks.

We took pictures of our achievement written out in the dirt, and I realized this was officially the longest hiking trip I had ever completed. Chilly attempted to hide her laughter – I imagine having two thru-hikes worth of experience makes 100 miles seem trivial. About 50 feet down the trail another marker was written in the middle of the trail, "100", this time in small stones. Then another a few hundred feet from that.

"Well, one of them is probably right…"

But it didn't really matter, what importance does the accuracy of a 100-mile marker have when your real goal is another 2092 miles north?

• • •

After coming down Albert Mountain, we crossed a highway, then headed straight back up another mountain and began looking for a place to make camp for the evening. Thankfully, this mountain wasn't nearly as brutal as Albert. Numerous flat spaces lining the trail as it made switchbacks up the hill. We picked a nice spot, slightly hidden from the trail by a mound of rock and soil, sheltered beneath the trees.

I staked out the corners of my tent, inflated my bright yellow sleeping pad, and laid it out on top of my unpitched tent to bath in the setting sun. Chilly joined me and we snacked together on chocolates and jerky until it was time for bed. She returned to her tent, and I finished erecting my own by placing trekking poles into the peak thus supporting the tent and forcing open the base to provide plenty of free space. I had room in this tent to store my pack and swim around in all my other gear. I was in heaven.

Early the next morning, before the sun had risen, I awoke to the pitter patter of rain. Thunder rolled on the horizon.

Chilly was already awake in her own tent. We knew about the scheduled storm, it was set to continue through the morning. Once the rain picked up, we realized it wouldn't be reasonable to talk to each other from different tents without yelling, and we weren't about to break camp just to hike through a storm.

I called over to her tent, "Hey, I probably have enough room in mine for the both of us, you can bring your pad".

She replied, "Ok, bring your pack and stuff to mine so we have more space".

And so we made quick trips through the rain to move her into my tent and my gear into hers. Then the rain really started coming, and the storm was right overhead. It turned out we didn't have much to say after all; whatever needed saying before this point had already been discussed over our days walking together on the trail. As I pointed out earlier, thru-hiking seems to transcend the limits of time, and bonds seem to form all the faster because of it.

So there in that cramped space, we made our feelings known in relative silence against the backdrop of the storm.

● ● ●

The next day, our ninth on trail, was a relatively flat walk over 18 miles or so. Sauntering through the Nantahala Forest was a pleasant experience; spring just started to show its abundance in the plants and wildlife that surrounded us. The trail itself was well blazed and maintained. Much like the trail crews of Georgia, the North Carolina trail clubs appeared to value a clean trail devoid of blowdowns or overgrowth. This was much appreciated.

With our new adventure and new relationship, all seemed

right with the world.

Our goal for today was to summit Wayah Bald. At the top we would find a stone lookout tower and an excellent view. By the time we reached the tower, the afternoon light faded in the distance and we were treated to colorful skies which met rolling mountains at the horizon. Thanks to a labeled graphic inside the tower, we were able to pinpoint the various mountains over which we had hiked, and those which would come next. In particular, we got our first glance of the Smoky Mountains – including the highest point on the Appalachian Trail, Clingmans Dome. After drinking in our fill of the sights that surrounded us, we climbed down from the summit and made camp at the first flat space inside the woods.

The following day, began with a brisk 14 mile hike before ending at the Nantahala Outdoor Center (NOC) Basecamp, a complex that included both kayaking adventures and thru-hiker bunkrooms which dotted the hillside. The NOC gear shop sits right on a river which rushes through the complex, a restaurant is positioned across the road from the gear shop, and a bridge between the two leads across the river and into the dorms.

This place was awesome, but I wasn't able to fully appreciate the scope of it until after we had our fill of bar food. Beer and greasy food always induces a unique bliss after hiking long distances; especially true because of the work to earn it.

After dinner, we headed over to the shop. I had been dealing with a few blisters on my toes, so I went straight for the sock wall. I selected a pair of Injinji toe socks, at Chilly's suggestion, which would prevent hotspots more permanently than any other solution I had tried thus far. Leukotape works great, but it needs replacing every two weeks or so. Changing socks, on the other hand, proved a permanent solution to my problem.

I also had a few pieces of gear to get rid of, so next I headed to the hiker box. Although I didn't find anything here for myself,

I did deposit my loose-leaf AWOL guidebook after having replaced it with the PDF version on my phone. An unfamiliar hiker who saw me do this exclaimed in disbelief, "Why would you get rid of something like that?!"

I expect she found herself a new guidebook after I left the building.

We sat on one of the benches out by the road and called for the ride service provided by the cottage company where we had booked a one night stay. The decision to use a private cottage over a shared bunk room at basecamp was simple: more privacy and comfort for our first night off trail as a couple. Eventually the shuttle service arrived, drove us up the road a ways, and then dropped us off at the "cottage".

It quickly became clear this business was nothing more than a couple who had a spare house near their own. Fine, but not what we had expected from the guidebook where we found their number. It was a fair price, and had everything we needed. More importantly, it was warm, dry, and a place we could call our own for the evening.

The next day the rains began early, and picked up through the morning. After being dropped off back at basecamp, we spent the next couple of hours hanging out in the riverside restaurant deciding when to head out. The forecast predicted sub-freezing temperatures on the ridgeline, and thunderstorms all afternoon. We almost went anyway, but after much deliberation, took our first day off – a *zero* day, meaning zero miles walked.

After our earlier decision to skip the bunkhouse on night one, we opted to save money and go for it on night two. To my surprise, it was also private (only because it didn't fill up), clean, and had everything we needed. Unfortunately, a large group of bikers were also staying at basecamp that night and partying long after hiker midnight (the time when the sun goes down and thru-hikers get sleepy). That made me a bit grumpy, but this is what you can expect in such a popular location.

●●●

Climbing out of Basecamp after our first zero demanded more than we were ready to give. Straight up the mountain, no time for a warm up, no sir. Let the huffing and puffing commence.

But the view from our perch at the top was worth it; from there we could look out over the Nantahala Gorge, still blanketed in a light fog only now being chased off by the morning sun. Taking it all in, both the gorgeous view and the rush of adrenaline after waking up to a steep climb, we were reinvigorated for whatever the day might hold.

As we learned while walking along the ridgeline, it was the right decision to stay put through the storm. Not only did we dodge a heavy downpour and lightning, but here on the mountain the morning had also brought a heavy frost which coated the tents and had frozen the water bottles belonging to those who skipped town. One hiker feared his water filter had frozen in the night, which if true, would render it non-functional. I say "if" because there is no way of knowing with the type of filter he was carrying. He would have no choice but to return to town and replace it or risk giardia exposure.

Up to this point, I had been using a Sawyer filter like the one used by this fellow hiker; but, while light and convenient because of its ability to screw onto any plastic bottle from which you could filter as you drank, the Sawyer is terribly slow compared to what Chilly and I were using now. She had started the trail with a Katadyn BeFree, and I was sold on the model as soon as I witnessed its flow rate – I had picked one up along with my new socks at the NOC. This filter is attached to a strong, but light bag which could be filled in any stream or trickle along the trail. The filter then screws onto the bag, and you could squeeze water through the filter at a rate of about one liter in ten seconds. Having previously used only the traditional pump filters, and then the Sawyer, this thing was the bee's knees.

We had about two days left in North Carolina before we hit the border with Tennessee where we would then walk along this border through the peaks of the Great Smoky Mountains National Park. Having gained our first sight of Clingmans Dome and the Smoky Mountains just days earlier, and about to reach Fontana Dam at the base of the park itself, I was awash in nostalgia. The park has been a fixture in my life since childhood, and my first backpacking trip on the Appalachian Trail had launched from the shelter at Fontana Dam just two years earlier.

MY FIRST NIGHTS ON THE APPALACHIAN TRAIL

> *"Carry as little as possible, but choose that little with care."* –Earl Shaffer, first AT thru-hiker

Two years prior to starting my Appalachian Trail thru-hike, I completed 79 miles through the Smoky Mountains heading northbound (NOBO) from Fontana Dam. Leaving my car in the parking lot at the Fontana Dam visitor's center, I walked about ten minutes southbound (SOBO) on the Appalachian Trail to reach a shelter called the Fontana Hilton. This shelter is basically a small barn in shape, technically having four walls with central doorways on either side. I expected solitude, but it turned out I had plenty of company; not humans, mind you, just the small critters whose scampering kept me awake most of the night

As a section-hiker, I was limited to just seven nights on the trail. I would walk the first half alone, then meet my family at Clingmans Dome where they would join me for the eight mile section from there to Newfound Gap. Here they would pick up the other car and head back to town while my brother and I would finish the other half of the Smokies.

It was a fitting place to do my first serious miles on the AT since I had first learned about the trail, and about thru-hiking more generally, in this park.

The first day was a big one, about 11 miles and 3500 feet of vertical elevation up to Mollies Ridge Shelter. I spent all day making my way up to the ridgeline, weaving back and forth through endless switchbacks in the oppressive summer heat. Regardless of the struggle, being both out of shape and having the most difficult section on day one, I thoroughly enjoyed myself. This climb exemplifies one of my favorite types of hiking: the further you go, the more you can see of where you have been. To look back at Fontana Dam shrinking with every switchback makes you realize on an intellectual level how much work you're doing, never mind the burning legs and the sweat dripping from your forehead.

That night at the shelter was an educational experience for me. I shared it with another couple who were section-hiking the Smoky Mountains in addition to a SOBO thru-hiker who claimed to be in third place for the year (with only two SOBOs ahead of him). I thought that was an odd claim to make, but whatever floats your boat I guess. We talked into the evening about particular gear choices he had made, and his thoughts on the trail. I never miss the opportunity to pick the brain of an expert.

● ● ●

The first morning I woke up on the Smoky Mountains ridgeline I was feeling fresh and strong. I called ahead to my parents and let them know that I planned to pick up the pace and would be at Newfound Gap a day earlier than we had discussed.

This brings me to briefly address an opinion I hear frequently, that hikers should slow down lest they miss the beauty of it all. I counter that argument with what my head and heart tell me; that the faster I walk, the more my adrenaline pumps and the happier I feel, the more I can take in and appreciate with my heightened senses, and that almost nothing in this world makes me smile more brightly than a brisk walk through the mountains. Some would say "smiles not miles," but I say to them "more miles makes more smiles," as I would happily put in four times the effort to see but twice the novelty.

Chilly would put it more simply, "have you ever driven through the countryside at three miles per hour and thought you were going too fast to take it all in?" Of course not.

The next day, I was due to summit Rocky Top – the subject of a bluegrass song that I heard often as a kid. I looked forward to the bald peak from which I would get my first 360° view of the park. It was late morning by the time I got to the final saddle and subsequent climb to its peak. A long, straight, and steep path to the top, it's a common day-hike and is strewn with places to sit along its length. I firmly fastened a trekking pole in each hand and charged up the mountain, pacing my breathing with my stride. For whatever reason, that climb stands out to this day as an exemplary instance of what I will call "hiker clarity".

Hiker clarity: a state of mental calm and euphoria produced by a mix of endorphins and a feeling of oneness with nature. Perhaps what Emerson would have called "the tyranny of the present".

When I'm backpacking, I sometimes reach this state of empty, mental clarity; which, when sustained over long distances, is incredibly effective at creating an enveloping notion of freedom. Like a flow state combined with endorphins and pristine scenery. Few other activities have the potential to generate both short and long term happiness in my experience.

At the top of the mountain I was overtaken with a sense of exuberance. I could see out in every direction, back to the places I had been and forward to the places I would soon go. I took my time here, and soaked in a freedom that I had hitherto been deprived.

Later, when I met my family at Clingmans Dome, we would set off together on an eight mile section to Newfound Gap. By the time I got to Clingmans Dome, the rain clouds were starting to settle in so we quickly set off to get under tree cover. This section is relatively flat, but has plenty of rocks and roots to act as tripping hazards. The trail here winds through a pine forest for most of the way, and the mixture of pine scents and fresh rain permeated our afternoon. My parents had packed sandwiches, and we huddled together under a particularly dense tree as we hid from the rain and ate our lunch.

Once we got back to their car at Newfound Gap, we bid them farewell and headed toward that old familiar brown sign where my initial attraction to the Appalachian Trail had first begun all those years ago. Giving the sign a gentle pat in greeting, Brian and I set off on our own up the steep, rocky path to Charlie's Bunion. Section-hikers in the Smoky Mountains need to book the shelters they will use ahead of time, and tonight was the one night where we were forced to stay in a non-AT shelter due to capacity limits. This meant we would have to hike down from the ridgeline almost 4000 feet tonight, and back up as much in the morning. In addition, this would be a 17 mile day for Brian, and 21 for me. Big miles for people who were not used to hiking every day.

Coming down from the ridgeline, we went from dense pine forest to low lying bush and sparse tree cover just as the rain set in. Kephart Shelter was our goal that evening, and it quickly became my favorite shelter – remaining so even after thru-hiking the entire Appalachian Trail. The shelter's placement, immediately next to a rushing river, combined with the rain resulting in a soothing melody as we fell asleep. In addition, it sits at the foot of the mountains, surrounded by rock and tall trees, giving it the eerie allure of a deep dark forest from some fairy tale.

The following morning we took off early knowing we would have a big day ahead of us. Starting with a rousing climb up to the Appalachian Trail, we set our sights on a shelter about 14 miles north. As luck would have it, we had a day filled with exposed ridgelines and generally beautiful views. However, the fun was cut short by terrible storms and reduced visibility.

Although I tried to prepare Brian as best I could, it turned out his waterproofing situation was far from adequate. As this was Brian's first real backpacking trip, he was using mostly hand-me-down gear including an external frame backpack from the '60s. By the time we had reached the shelter that evening, he and his gear had soaked completely through. Even the sleeping bag was damp.

Hypothermia is a real risk in the Smoky Mountains, even through the summer months. After filtering some water out of a shallow puddle, we set to making a fire and getting Brian dried out. We hung as much as we could in front of the fire, and I gave Brian some spare clothes and my puffy jacket. Brian still recounts that as the day he learned more about backpacking than any time before or since. For better or worse, the rest of our hike was somewhat less eventful.

Overall, this trip was a great learning experience for both my brother and me. For my part, I tested several pieces of gear which would become standbys for my upcoming thru-hike including tights rather than underwear to protect from ticks and plant irritants, trail runners, and the knowledge that I wanted to avoid sleeping in shelters if at all possible. This was by far my longest trip to date, and I knew now more than ever that a thru-hike would be in my future.

I was ready.

INTO THE SMOKY MOUNTAINS

"The knapsack of custom falls off his back with the first step he makes into these precincts. Here is sanctity which shames our religions, and reality which discredits our heroes. Here we find nature to be the circumstance which dwarfs every other circumstance, and judges like a god all men that come to her. We have crept out of our close and crowded houses into the night and morning, and we see what majestic beauties daily wrap us in their bosom." –Ralph Waldo Emerson

Two years after my first overnight trip through the Smoky Mountains with my brother, I was now approaching the front door to her steep hills once more. It felt a little bit like returning home. My nostalgia began boiling over, and I couldn't help but share it with everyone around me.

The night before heading into the Smoky Mountains, Chilly and I stayed at the Fontana Hilton. Although it both sounds like a hotel and comes complete with a shower block, the Fontana Hilton is nothing more than an AT shelter on the edge of Fontana Lake. It does include fire circles, benches, an ice cold swimming hole, and a nearby visitors center. The first time I stayed here I did so alone, but today the shelter was packed.

Our first order of business was to restock for the trip into the Smokies. Our next stop would be Gatlinburg just under 40 miles north, so we just needed to top up. Although the visitor's center has a hiker box and a few snack options, the nearby Fontana village contains a small grocery store and, as it turned out, an ice cream shop too. We hadn't expected to go to Fontana Village at all; but after speaking a while with a pair of kindly volunteer workers, they offered to give us a ride after they closed up shop. My first real hitch couldn't have been better: riding in a pickup bed through the pine forest with wind blowing through my hair, enjoying both the perfect weather and our new relationship.

After our restock, and a quick hitch back to the Fontana Hilton, we spent the evening socializing and doing a little swimming (well not me, that water was painfully cold, but Chilly got in for a few minutes before rushing toward the hot showers). By this point in the trail, we had already made the decision to avoid sleeping in shelters as much as possible. Just as well, as the shelter would be packed full tonight. Instead, we found a nice grassy patch just a little further up the trail where we could pitch our tents.

Tonight, as with several nights prior, we would be sharing my Lightheart Gear Solo tent and using her smaller Tarptent Aeon Li to store gear. I don't know if you have ever attempted to put two adults in a one person tent, but I would not recommend doing so for any length of time. Needless to say, we would be needing a two person tent if this was the new way of things.

The next morning we were met with a bright, warm day as we set off towards the dam. The Appalachian Trail follows the road across Fontana Dam before winding its way up into the mountains. We took some time at the dam taking photos. It really is picturesque, and Chilly is a civil engineer with a particular love for water, so she felt right at home.

Ahead of us, the 3500 foot climb onto the ridgeline appeared menacing. I remembered it distinctly from the first time, when I was out of shape and just starting my trip. Even had I put a few more weekend trips under my belt, I still wouldn't have been in the shape that I was now. There isn't anything quite like hiking every single day for two weeks straight to get you in shape (at least that's what I thought until I had 500 miles in, and then 1000, and then 2000).

What had taken a whole day the first time round, we knocked out by lunchtime. Then we pushed on to the next shelter as well. This first day in the Smokies, including the hardest section in the park, was also our first 20+ mile day. We had planned to stop at 20 miles even; but with no flat space to camp, we ended up walking an extra 4.5 miles that day – those last few miles were probably some of the longest and hardest miles on trail (subjectively speaking).

On the second day in the Smokies, we met a family of four out for a day-hike on the Appalachian Trail. The father asked if we were thru-hiking, and I confirmed. I told the kids about my first seeing the AT around their age, and hearing thru-hikers talk about their experiences. I told them to enjoy it because they will look back and maybe be inspired just like I was. The dad couldn't have been more thrilled; and I experienced the satisfaction of paying it forward, if only just a little.

● ● ●

Walking along this rolling ridgeline on a sunny afternoon, Chilly and I got into an argument that threatened to drive us apart. Of course it was over something foolish, but looking back now it's understandable.

People who are raised on opposite sides of the Earth, who have experienced different upbringings and educations and who, despite speaking the same language, have different accents and sometimes surprisingly different uses for the same words and phrases should be expected to experience some minor cultural clashes upon interacting in such a continuous, fluid, and physically stressful environment. No one could be faulted for simple gaffs. Most were even the source of laughter and delight at learning some new way of thinking.

Yet ultimately, several such gaffs were not taken well by one party or the other. This built up, pressurizing like a geyser. Until finally, one day, the pressure burst through and we each said things we didn't mean. It was here, in a park filled with such natural beauty and good memories for me, that Chilly and I hit the one and only road bump in our relationship. And so we separated at a particularly grimy watering hole on the side of some mountain in the Smokies.

I marched back up the hill with the vigor and enthusiasm of an enraged elephant and left her standing there alone. I huffed and puffed down the trail. In my anger, I argued out loud with the version of her that only existed in my imagination. I marched in lockstep with the tip tap of my trekking poles for several miles until I had blown off all the steam.

And then I sat, and I ate my Snickers, and I waited. The "hangry" hiker that argued over something so stupid and petty was left there on that log, waiting. Then, after some time, Chilly walked around the corner after having blown off her own steam and a better partner rose from the log to greet her.

All was forgiven. Nothing was lost.

We could have continued on our own that day, but we got over ourselves and were all the stronger for having done so. Never again would such silliness come between us.

• • •

On the summit of Rocky Top, I took a moment to delight Chilly with my rendition of Good Ole' Rocky Top, the song I learned as a boy. My singing voice is nothing to write home about, but we had a laugh all the same. We also took advantage of this bald summit, and its vanishingly small cell phone signal, to call ahead and make reservations at one of the motels on the outskirts of Gatlinburg. We planned to stay the night before heading into town at Tri-Corner Shelter which lies between Clingmans Dome and Newfound Gap, then catch a shuttle from Newfound Gap down from the mountain the next morning.

I've been to Clingmans Dome a number of times before, but

never on a clear day. Lucky for us, the day we arrived couldn't have been more perfect. From atop the cement tower with its spiral ramp, you can see over the emerald mountains in every direction, rolling like green waves as far as you can see.

As the highest point on the Appalachian trail, Clingmans Dome marks the point from which the trail must only go downhill all the way to Maine; yes, the hard part must be behind us now!

If only we had known what grueling adventures were to come after the Mason-Dixon Line...

Down from Clingmans Dome we came, heading to Tri-Corner Shelter – a beautiful, secluded haven deep in the pine forest. Little did we know, this picturesque campsite would be the start of one of the worst days on the entire trail.

That night we woke up to nearly flooded tents. I had chosen that night to try Chilly's Thermarest foam pad for the first time, rather than sticking with my much better insulated inflatable pad. I woke up freezing and heard the grumbling coming from Chilly's tent located across a flat clearing. She had woken up dry, but kicked the side of her tent's bathtub down and was soon floating along with all her gear. I had remained dry in the night, but soon packed up in the pouring rain. She left camp as soon as she could, the risk of hypothermia already setting in. I was slower, as usual, but I moved out quickly as I could – both to stay warm and to catch up.

We had planned to meet a shuttle at Newfound Gap, just five miles from our campsite. We arrived early, the rain hadn't stopped. Without the effort of hiking to keep us warm, we were forced to take shelter inside the only place we could – the bathroom block. By the time the shuttle was due, and we had stepped out of our hiding spot, a large group of other hikers had begun to amass. It became increasingly clear as we waited 15, then 30, then 45 minutes out in the pouring rain that our shuttle wasn't coming. Finally, someone checked their phone and found that the shuttles had been canceled – the road up to Newfound Gap was flooded and too dangerous for cars to come.

With our numbers approaching 40, we again took shelter from the freezing rain inside the bathroom blocks. Now packed far past capacity, we contacted the park service to determine our best option for getting down to Gatlinburg. Men and women alike shared these spaces, any thoughts about gender separation were brushed definitively to the side as we were faced with a growing number of safety concerns. We were ready to just walk the 15 miles to town; but the park service demanded we stay put.

A chill rattled in my spine, and Chilly said my lips had gone blue. I pulled my puffy jacket and raincoat a little tighter.

I was fine, just completely miserable.

We waited like this for a total of six hours, being reassured several times that the park service would come. Finally, it wasn't the park service but a young kid who poked his head into the men's restroom. He said he had a pickup truck and was headed down the mountain as soon as he picked up his brother, and that he could take three or four of us with them.

To my surprise, the dozens of hikers who stood closer than us to the door parted like the Red Sea, and someone waved us forward – everyone knew we had been waiting the longest. I knew in that moment that thru-hikers truly are a family, and we'll always look out for each other when the going gets tough.

So we all piled into the truck and picked up the driver's brother, five of us squashed in across the back seat, including me cuddled up on Chilly's lap. His brother turned out to be the thru-hiker who went by "Baby", a plump and jovial chap we had just met the day before.

Our trip down the mountain was illuminating. The rivers

were flooding over their banks onto the road, and trees were down by the sides of the road. The reason for the warnings expressed by the park services were instantly apparent. About four miles from town we came to a fallen tree across the road, far too big to move by hand, and impossible to drive around. We piled out of the truck and continued on foot, thanking the driver and promising to send help. There was a visitor center about a mile from where we had left the driver and a group of firefighters had just finished working on a fallen log when we came upon them. After we told them about the stranded truck just a mile up the road, they hopped in their truck and headed up the mountain.

Our exploits at Newfound Gap made the local news that night; we happily watched it from our warm beds.

● ● ●

Gatlinburg would prove to be our next test in the relationship. Chilly came down with norovirus the morning after we first arrived in Gatlinburg. Being packed in a restroom with dozens of other dirty hikers is a great way to spread this virulent illness, but we had little choice in the matter. To complicate matters, my parents would visit us for the first time on trail. While their visit was a welcome reunion, it came only one week into our relationship. Chilly wound be forced to meet my parents while feeling completely under the weather. We both knew this was a little early, but this would be our lot. After introductions, Chilly isolated herself in the motel room while I spent the rest of the time with my parents.

Then came the decision to stay another day or not. This was not in the plan, and we both agreed that many people would have hiked on and just hoped to rendezvous later. Instead, I decided to stay with her, a decision that felt very much like a statement on our relationship at the time. It demonstrated to my parents the degree to which I was willing to risk my thru-hike pace for my new partner, something they would later tell me led them to realize how serious it was. This may seem like an obvious decision now, but such things are far from cut and dry during a thru-hike.

In summation, Chilly didn't have a very good time in Gatlinburg – but meeting my parents actually made it better. I was happy to see them and be treated to some great food too.

However, the nostalgia I felt for the Gatlinburg of my youth was somewhat undermined by the degree to which it has become a tourist destination. The streets were flooded with obese tourists who would never even step foot in the mountains; and to appease their need for entertainment, the town had been overrun with gaudy shops, time shares, unhealthy food stalls, and mini-golf for the more "adventurous" crowd.

Maybe it was partially my fault as well. I had certainly overhyped this destination by sharing memories colored by the magical haze of youth. But all I could remember were the mountains. This, combined with her illness, left Chilly with a bad impression of Gatlinburg.

That being said, Gatlinburg was something of a turning point for us – and for me in particular. I happily sent home more than six pounds of gear, handing my parents a black garbage bag full of stuff.

Their eyes nearly popped out of their heads at the sight of me Marie Kondo-ing what precious little I had.

Their worry and concern that I had overdone it was clear, but I had made the first major step on my journey towards a significantly lower pack weight. It brought me considerable joy to reduce my burden as my trail confidence built.

We would also leave Gatlinburg more certain of our relationship than before, and we haven't looked back since. Moreover, Chilly had arranged to receive her two person tent at Damascus Virginia two weeks ahead.

It was settled, we were moving in together having known each other for only two weeks.

MAKING THE BEST OF IT

> *"Live in each season as it passes; breathe the air, drink the drink, taste the fruit, and resign yourself to the influence of the earth." –Henry David Thoreau*

My parents helped us return to the trail from Gatlinburg, driving up the familiar road to Newfound Gap and returning once more to the brown trail marker now so symbolic of my desire to hike the Appalachian Trail. Spring was making a strong advance by this point and the fresh fragrance of it was on the wind.

We quickly made our way through the rest of the Smokies, just one night and then out the other side. The Great Smoky Mountains National Park truly is a national treasure. It contains more biological diversity than anywhere else in the country, including a large black bear population, and all of it in a relatively small patch of land. In addition to our first black bear, we also saw an assortment of salamanders and lizards of all colors, the most common of which was the orange spotted newt. This area was also our first run-in with blooming mountain laurels, their pure white petals littering the ground like freshly fallen snow. In truth, these were just the early bloomers; we were about a month off from their peak season during which large sections of the trail would be lined on either side. I hear peak season is a sight to behold, though I have never yet timed it right in the Smokies.

Immediately after descending from the Smoky Mountain range, we came to Standing Bear Hostel. Really more like a small village containing bunk rooms, laundry, and an honor system restock room. Standing Bear shouldn't be missed. Just by chance, we ran into a group of guys whom we had met back at the Fontana Hilton. In particular I want to mention Tex, I'm sure I don't have to tell you where he's from. Tex was one of the nicest guys I met on the trail, which makes me kick myself even harder knowing that I had made an ass of myself by poking fun of people with fifty pound packs right in front of him. You see, Tex was strong as an ox and carried a pack size to prove it. Complete with a folding camp chair, he claimed a kit with supreme comfort and style.

Who am I to disagree? I would remiss to ignore the fact that I was just a bit jealous when we passed him in his camp chair watching the setting sun just a few days later.

Our next major stop was Hot Springs, North Carolina, a quaint little town right on the trail. We had read in the AWOL guide that Elmer's Hostel (actually called the Sunnybank Inn, but Elmer is the star of that show) was one of the most unique hostels on the AT, so we called ahead and booked our spot. However, we had to arrive before 3 PM and we had quite a few miles ahead of us.

The highlight of this section was Max Patch, a 300+ acre flat bald with panoramic views. An easy day-hike from the parking lot, the summit of Max Patch is quite a popular place with the locals, and the trail magic here is abundant. This area was first cleared in the 1800's for pasture land, and ongoing maintenance is required to keep the bald as it is. We took our time, relaxing in the sun and enjoying the multiple rounds of fresh fruit and trail snacks brought to us by trail angels interested in hearing our story.

Unfortunately, Chilly was still recovering from norovirus and having a rough go of it on the day we were due in town. We knew she was no longer contagious long before we interacted with anyone, a fact that would be confirmed by the local clinic. Even so, she was too weak to hike these distances. About four miles from Hot Springs, she decided to set up her tent and have a nap while I pushed forward to secure our spot. We looked back on that decision almost immediately, and I know I shouldn't have left her by herself in that state. But as luck would have it, a friendly passerby in a car would happen upon her tent, which was set up near a stone drive, and offer her a ride back to town.

Sure to never miss a mile, Chilly would catch a shuttle back the next day and complete the small section she had skipped the day before.

Elmer's hostel is our favorite on the trail for a number of reasons. The building itself predates the advent of thru-hiking, and its decorative style included antiquities from around the world as if to accentuate this fact. Elmer himself was quite the caretaker, and as a professor and world traveler, he was also quite the conversationalist. Additionally, the house itself was outfitted with a music room containing an assortment of instruments for the guests to use. Chilly happily took advantage of this. For my own part, there was a small library of hiking and philosophy books which I rummaged through eventually finding a book called "Backpacking with the Saints" which provided interesting insight on backpacking as a spiritual endeavor; I was particularly drawn to the section on lightweight backpacking and minimalism.

That evening I sat in the music room reading while Chilly played the guitar and sang to me. In the morning and evenings, Elmer made and served a family meal with all the hikers discussing their adventures and the life they had temporarily left behind.

If you have the opportunity, I urge you to stay at Elmer's as the time spent there won't soon be forgotten.

We didn't get far out of Hot Springs before the norovirus caught up with me. I thought I was in the clear since I didn't get it alongside Chilly.

We had made our campsite on a beach by the river just outside of town. But by the morning I knew I wouldn't make it far. Chilly headed back into town to grab us some sandwiches and I slept it off by the river. That evening, I tried to eat what little I could. The sandwiches didn't go well, so I tried a pop tart instead.

Big mistake. The result was vomiting still unchewed pop tarts, along with the contents of my stomach, as far away from the water source as I could make it.

Probably not far enough, honestly.

We tried it again the next day. Cold and miserable in the downpour that day, I stumbled along doing all I could to stay upright. Gingerly making my way down a set of stairs, my shoe caught the edge of a rock and I stumbled forward a step before falling flat on my face. I was livid, drained, cold and wet with the shakes from either the cold or the illness – I couldn't be certain. Never had I fallen like this, so uncontrolled and clumsy. I should have just stayed in my tent.

We set up camp early, and got me into some dry clothes. I could barely change them myself, Chilly did most of the work for me. I was in pitiful shape.

But the next day, and the day after, I felt great. We were approaching Erwin, Tennessee which is where the norovirus outbreak first started, we had been hearing about it almost since the start of the trail. My parents were set to meet us again in Erwin to take us into town to restock and have a night in a hotel. It was good to see them again and they treated us to some great Mexican food. However, Chilly's Gatlinburg experience was about to play itself out again in Erwin, this time with me being sick and her unaffected. I spent the next two days in the hotel room with frequent trips to the bathroom. Chilly took some comical video of me on the day we finally decided to head out, laying on the bed fully clothed, including shoes, complaining like a lazy schoolboy pleading for a sick day.

Overall we lost seven days to sickness, but this would luckily be the last of it. We did all we could to isolate ourselves from others, especially by completely avoiding hostels and shelters when we knew we were sick. The problem is that it hits so suddenly. We never expected it to come and go like it did, and we hope that we did not cause others to get sick as well. But this is what makes it so difficult to stop an outbreak of norovirus on the trail.

•••

After I had fully recovered, we slowly started to regain our confidence and increase our daily miles. Still skirting the Tennessee/North Carolina border, we eventually came to the Roan Highlands – the longest stretch of grassy bald on the AT. Areas like this quickly became my favorite on the trail, unique with their open vistas and windswept hills rolling out to the horizon. We walked for miles on bald mountain after bald mountain and, for the first time, could see other hikers over a mile ahead on the trail we would soon walk ourselves. Mountains like these were alien to our trail experience this far, reminding us more of the pictures from Maine than of the south's green hills. These highlands were the last we would see of the Tennessee border before finally dropping fully into North Carolina and heading toward Virginia.

Over the next six days we did about 115 miles to get to our next major location: Damascus, Virginia. Near the halfway point of this tramp, we stumbled upon a little sign in the woods. It pointed down a well maintained side trail and read, "Scotty's Budget Solar Hostel". Thinking we were nearing the end of our day anyway, and being drawn to brown signs in the woods such as I was, we decided to check it out.

Appearing suddenly from the pine covered slopes, Scotty's is like a little oasis in the woods. He provides microwave pizzas, trips to the local grocery store, complimentary piano music in the evening, and a hot tub.

A HOT TUB! Quite the find for just stumbling through the woods.

We enjoyed the evening thoroughly. Scotty played the piano while I sat in the hot tub, finally able to rest my weary bones in this godsend of hot, massaging goodness. Being a couple, we were presented with the suite above the bunkroom which was accessed through an attic hatch. Private and cozy, we enjoyed our budget stay without reservation. The following morning we set out again on our road to Damascus. Fresh and reinvigorated, my mental focus returned squarely to my new goal: further reducing the contents of my pack to the bare essentials.

● ● ●

Minimalism is both the chicken and the egg in many spiritual practices; a method and a result of concentrated effort aimed at better understanding self and happiness. Backpacking is itself an actionable form of minimalism; and if you're reading this, I probably don't need to tell you about the physical and mental benefits of hiking.

Somewhere between Springer Mountain and Virginia, I realized that losing pack weight was about more than simply lightening the load. After that first major gear dump, I quickly came to appreciate the sparseness of my kit upon exploding it into the tent each night. Less to keep track of, less to lose. This eased my mind more than the reduced weight did by itself.

Soon I came to realize that this sort of active minimalism was both intellectually satisfying, like solving a puzzle, as well as mentally and physically soothing. I donated to hiker boxes until I had nothing left I could give away.

I think the approach to ultralight backpacking should progress, if it does at all, in lockstep with backpacking experience. Belden C. Lane, in his book "Backpacking with the Saints", said:

"Packing for the trip is an exercise in values clarification."

I couldn't agree more.

It was an experience of unburdening; physically at first, and mentally by extension.

I could no longer forget or misplace anything when I packed up in the morning because I only had a handful of things left, and they all had a specific place in my pack. The moment anything was ever out of place I could sense it in the way my pack rode.

Simple, or natural, living is not itself the producer of happiness; but, by producing scarcity in people otherwise overrun with modern abundance, nature creates a void into which happiness can be forged through the pleasures of existing successfully in challenging environments. By training under such conditions, I find that any fear of the unknown, or of being stranded without, seems to evaporate.

Minimalism, especially as a path rather than a destination, taught me just how little is required for happiness or satisfaction. The focus of minimalism is to realize you can be happy and at peace with less; and, that having more is often a major contributor to stress, greed, and other negative emotions. Being drawn toward simplicity: it's the way of the thru-hike, and it's the key to minimalism.

FINDING COMMUNITY IN THE WILDERNESS

Call me Raiden.

The fact that I'm a scientist was something I chose not to bring up unless a question or statement from one of my hiking companions brought it up. On the trail I was just Raiden.

The trappings of my old life, which I had worked so hard to achieve, were at once thrown out as if meaningless. Almost as if the trail itself had given me permission, I allowed myself to be simple again. A form of compartmentalization, not self-deprecating or aggrandizing; extracted, as it were, from the rat race in which we willingly participate. My very ambition would find itself a third party to the adventurer within.

Although I am, and always will be, a scientist at heart; I had allowed myself in the span of a month to become a new man entirely, at least for the duration of this adventure. It was not a conscious decision – but rather a gift provided by the trail itself, or the time and space it created just by way of its very existence.

•••

Just inside the Virginia border is the little trail town of Damascus. Each year Damascus hosts the Appalachian Trail's largest celebration of the thru-hiking community: Trail Days. This three-day event brings hikers together from the length of the Appalachian Trail, even thru-hikers from years past, along with an assortment of vendors, artists and musicians, and members of the trail town community at large.

On average, 50% of would-be thru-hikers will have quit by this point. Chilly joked that meant one of us had to go home.

I promptly pointed out where she could hitch a ride to the nearest airport.

Gonna take more than violent illness, blisters, and sprained ankles to keep us down. What's a little hypothermia between lovers?

Our first time to Damascus we were about a week early for this event, we would just be passing through for now.

Stopping into one of the local shops, I was greeted by one of the best instances of the trail providing actual gear that I would see the entire trip. For a week or two, I had been thinking about buying a sleeping bag liner and planned to look for one in Damascus. Though I had never used one, I had realized that this thin layer of silk might be the perfect amount of insulation during the sweltering summer months. It would also keep my sleeping bag clean, and could be washed easier than down.

Low and behold, a hiker box placed in the very shop where I was looking to buy a liner contained a nearly new Big Agnes silk liner just for me! Sure it was used, and had a small hole where its previous owner had kicked through it in the middle of the night; but otherwise, it was perfect.

The town buzzed with everyone preparing for the biggest event of the year. In parallel and stark contrast, the mood in the thru-hiking community was significantly dampened by recent events that took place less than 100 miles north of Damascus. It had been rumored earlier, but confirmed for us in Damascus, that a group of thru-hikers were assaulted in the middle of the night by a madman with a knife. Unfortunately, this led to the severe injury of one, and the death of another. Stronghold. A combat veteran who had survived combat in the Middle East, and had made it this far through his healing journey on the AT, was cut down in his home country, on public lands, where we should feel safe and free from man-made violence. Rest in peace Stronghold.

At the time, the killer was still at large. We would be hiking into the area where it had happened in just a few days, and had concerns about our own safety. Lucky for us, and for the community as a whole, he would soon be caught and we didn't have to change course or pace. Thru-hiking requires accepting a degree of reliance on the kindness of strangers, and this was put at risk for everyone. Things like this are rare on the AT, but not completely unheard of. But it's never easy, and can never be accepted as just another risk of the trail.

● ● ●

Our plan was to restock at Damascus this time through, continue north as far as we could, then meet up with my parents who would drive us back to Trail Days and enjoy the weekend with us. This first time in Damascus we stayed in a donations only hostel run by one of the many churches that line the streets of this small town. It was a fine place to stay, and we ran into several of our trail friends from the first quarter of the trail.

The choices for housing in Damascus created a bit of a "choose your own adventure" scenario for hikers. Ours was a quiet place, being run by the church and all; but thru-hikers could have quite the opposite experience just down the road a little way at the Broken Fiddle. This hostel, which is run by a friendly group of people who invited us to their movie night even though we weren't staying, is known for a party atmosphere that welcomes all. A much needed black sheep in this overly religious town.

Our return trip to Damascus a week later was a much higher energy environment. The town was abuzz with outdoors enthusiasts of all ages and experience levels. Vendor tents ran the length of the town, a stage was set up for performers, and food trucks lined the venue making for a small arena in the park where it all took place. Additionally, the various churches were putting on services that included free sewing and gear repairs, as well as foot massages. We took full advantage of the sewing station by having them repair my new sleeping bag liners, and we also asked the nice old ladies to affix the straps of our fanny packs so that the buckles wouldn't ever slide. The foot massages were decidedly less useful, as the Baptist Church which offered them was much more interested in conversion than comfort.

After having reduced the volume of my gear, shedding the extra warm layers required in the Smoky Mountains; I hunted through the vendor area for a new ultralight backpack. I tested packs and asked questions. I entered all the drawings that were offered by the gear vendors and actually won a nice Granite Gear pack. Unfortunately, it would not be the replacement I was looking for.

Finally, I found a booth on the outskirts of the event which had what I needed. A new cottage brand called Nashville Pack and Equipment Company was debuting their frameless, hip-belt-less, lightskin pack. I fell in love instantly. I had already settled on losing the hip belt after my Osprey Exos had been digging into and bruising my hips for hundreds of miles. But the thing that really sold me about this pack was its running vest style harness, and its sub-one pound weight. Although they wouldn't let me buy the display packs, I did get in on their next shipment and would receive this pack a couple hundred miles up the trail.

The main attraction of Trail Days, assuming you're not a gear vendor, is meeting up with friends from the trail and meeting like-minded hikers from years past. The culminating event is a giant parade through town complete with thru-hikers segmented and led by a banner or sign displaying the year they completed the trail. I had fully expected to partake in this event, but somehow didn't receive the memo about the tradition of thrift store cross-dressing during the parade. One of my most notable memories is of Showstopper, a show tunes singing friend we made in Tennessee, and involves him masterfully indulging the trench coat and Speedo look with an abundant and contagious pride and enthusiasm.

Trail Days should certainly be witnessed by all thru-hikers at some point; there's really something for everyone – even a number of things I personally preferred to avoid. On that note, I want to address both the concerns and interest surrounding party culture on the trail.

The Appalachian Trail can really be whatever you make it, as long as what you want isn't an easy walk in the woods. This is the meaning behind the common adage to "hike your own hike". Likewise, if you get on the trail seeking to party, you will find it aplenty. If you get on the trail seeking solitude, you can have it. Just don't assume either of these situations will hold true 100% of the time. If you seek abstinence, I believe you will find the thru-hiking community unintrusive and respectful of your wishes.

Overall, our community is one of tolerance and acceptance of every approach to hiking, and to life in general. This is my own experience, I know it's not the only one by any means; but, I hope others have the same impression of our community as I have. If not, then at least that we can continue moving in this direction.

• • •

Trail days was fantastic. I believe my parents were also quite happy to see, and be involved with, our community on this level. They also took a day while in Virginia to see the Grayson Highlands which we had passed through just before they picked us up. The Grayson Highlands are a fantastic park that rises up from the valleys onto a plateau with wide pastures and bald mountains. It's the home to the famous wild painted ponies. These ponies are quite used to people, and are comfortable letting humans get relatively close for pictures even with new foals present. The downside to this region is that the ponies will happily bite through your pack or tent if given the opportunity. It's a bit of a shame that the Appalachian Trail passes through only a small corner of the Grayson Highlands, it's easily one of the prettiest areas of the south. I would very much like to return there one day and hike more of their trails.

After Trail Days, my parents dropped us off at the Big Red Barn restaurant where they had met us a few days earlier. We gave them our thanks and said our goodbyes before heading across the highway and down into the bush once more. We had walked about 500 miles by this point and we were starting to develop our "trail legs", being in peak physical shape after hiking daily. Feeling strong, we marched forward with renewed vigor after our time in town.

During our second trip to Damascus we had finally received our two-person tent in the mail, and had sent our single tents home with my parents. Our new home would be a bright yellow Lanshan 2 which stands out like a sore thumb against the dark green backdrop of the AT. Our yellow palace within a green tunnel.

To my dismay, the next heavy rain would teach me the meaning of splash back, the effect of rain drops splashing into puddles or hard packed dirt and, subsequently, into the tent itself. The first night experiencing this resulted in us scurrying about in the rain, naked in the dark, blind after forgetting to put my glasses on, trying to build walls from the leaves and debris that would protect our down sleeping bags from getting damp.

I guess this is the price you pay for love.

●●●

Our next destination would be the Virginia Triple Crown, a set of three mountainous ascents topped by unique rock formations. This area acts as a major hiking destination and achievement for those in and around Virginia.

Although we hadn't heard of the Virginia Triple Crown prior to reaching it, almost everyone familiar with the trail has heard of the most notable of the three: McAfee Knob.

Preceding McAfee knob on the trail heading northbound was the Dragon's Tooth. Making for an excellent day-hike, the Dragon's Tooth is a relatively easy climb from the south side heading north. The day-hiking trail terminates at the giant stone obelisk for which the trail gets its name. More adventurous hikers can then find their way up and around the base of the tooth to a crack between the rocks, allowing access to the very top of this unique natural structure. Others, less inclined to the heights, will find an open, flat setting at the base of the tooth. Perfect for lunch.

Those continuing onward past the obelisk, such as NOBO thru-hikers, then exit the tooth area down a much more difficult climb (even for thru-hikers who had developed their trail legs over the past several hundred miles). This side requires scampering over boulders, wedging yourself between rocks to slide carefully down to the next level, as well as some long drops down to ledges. This obstacle course was not for the faint of heart.

In between each peak in the Triple Crown lies five to ten miles of rolling expanse, then another steep climb to the next vantage point. Somewhere along this section we met a family of day-hikers enjoying their lunch. The teenage daughter happened to recognize Chilly from her video blog on YouTube.

I'm not sure whose face lit up more, Chilly's or the girl's.

"I'm video blogging too! I don't have many followers but it's still fun! How do you post from the trail? I hope to hike the whole trail one day too! What do you guys do when it rains!?"

I suppose she only stopped the inquisition to catch her breath! But Chilly handled it calmly and gave her some helpful advice to get started.

"Just do it for your friends, and for yourself. That's the key to good content."

I added, "And when it rains, you just have to keep walking. You get used to it eventually, just another feature of hiking really".

But the girl's eyes were fixated on Chilly, I don't think she even noticed I was there.

Soon enough we were on our way up the next mountain. Chilly was all smiles. I like to think she was inspiring the next generation, one kid at a time.

● ● ●

McAfee Knob is notable for being the single most photographed location on the Appalachian Trail. From its rocky precipice a vast ocean of green races all the way to the horizon. It's all but required for thru-hikers to pose for a picture on this triangle shaped outcropping, and we aimed to do so around sunset that day. The photos of this location make it seem like they are being taken from some distant location, perhaps another outcropping miles away. In reality, though no less beautiful, the area seen in these photos encompasses less than one to two hundred feet of rock before again being draped in dense tree cover. To our great pleasure, we were blessed with an orange and pink sunset settling just behind the knob, granting that iconic photograph sought by all.

After spending an hour or two enjoying the end of another fantastic day complete with a romantic sunset, we hurried down from the summit chased by the encroaching darkness. Our goal was about two miles down the mountain.

I have an affinity for night hiking, especially when the moon is high and bright in the sky. Though I would have liked to do more of it on the Appalachian Trail, we often settled in by nightfall. This was usually the safest option in the dense summer tree cover or the sometimes dangerous ridge walking.

As a side note, if you are so inclined, I would highly recommend giving night hiking a fair shake, and doing so without a headlamp for as long as possible to really adjust to the moonlight and allow for a more peaceful setting. Chilly thinks I'm crazy.

The next day we were set to climb Tinker Cliffs, the final point in the Virginia Triple Crown. From these, endless mountains can be observed while walking along the edge of the precipice for at least a mile before dropping back down to the valley.

Near this point in the trail, we stumbled upon the best trail magic of our entire trip. We were standing by the roadside attempting to hitch into town for a quick restock. As luck would have it, the trail angel "Longhorn" would pick us up while preparing to provide trail magic later the same day. We told him we just needed to find a grocery store, and hopefully somewhere to recharge our phones and backup batteries.

Immediately upon hearing that, and knowing it also meant we had been out for several days, he invited us back to his house for a shower and fresh food. He would offer us power, a hot shower, tales of his work on an AT maintenance crew before helping us back to the trail. He also handed us sandwiches to go!

A few hours later, we walked down the other side of the mountain from where Longhorn had left us; and there he sat, providing food and drinks to other thru-hikers, delighted as we were to meet again. His unconditional love of the trail and those who hike it exemplifies, at least in my mind, what our community is at its core and reminds me of what brings us all together.

I was exuberant the rest of the afternoon. We had another mountain to climb, but once we reached the top I exclaimed, "I'm going for a run now!" before jogging the remaining two miles downhill. I imagined that Chilly's eyes were rolling in her head, but she had seen me run on the trail before.

Sometimes when the weather is good, and I'm feeling great, I just have to run.

VIRGINIA IS FOR LOVERS

"In every walk with nature, one receives far more than he seeks." –John Muir

At this point in the trail our relationship was about a month old, but it felt far more serious than you might imagine; and only in the best of ways. A mathematician friend of ours who had been making an appearance on and off since Hiawassee, Platypus, remarked around this point that a thru-hike worth of time spent with your significant others would equate to more than a year of dating in the traditional sense. We were spending 24/7 together; more time than most married partners spend together, let alone couples who were just dating.

This made us feel like our act of "moving in together" wasn't rushed at all. And more to the point, everything was going perfectly for us.

The middle section of Virginia is long and low with rolling hills, but the common representation of this state as flat is wholly inaccurate. In addition, there is much beauty to observe during this time of the year when the northbound bubble arrives: an abundance of pink mountain laurels, white and purple trillium, flowering dogwood trees, and a wide array of other flowering plants. This variation in color helps break up the otherwise ubiquitous green that notoriously creates the "green tunnel" accounting for most of the southern ¾ of the AT.

Wildlife is also abundant here, including an assortment of colorful lizards, salamanders, and newts as well as mammals which range from small porcupines (which I first saw as one ran past our tent one evening) to white tailed deer and the famed black bear. Of these, black bear sightings were not uncommon for us, but it turns out we were lucky to see so many – many NOBOs still hadn't seen even one. Crossing paths with these gentle giants, when done with mutual respect, reminds us that we are but guests in another's house.

Many species of bird also flourished in this area of the trail, the most frequent of which were the ubiquitous "cheeseburger birds" (so nicknamed due to the sound of their song, otherwise named the black capped chickadee) and the ruffed grouse who's deep thumping noise penetrates the skull and resonates in your chest. Like little ninjas, this latter species has a knack for hiding in the brush alongside the AT and surprising the unsuspecting hiker just as they turn a bend. More than a few times I was startled almost to the point of jumping off trail.

As we sauntered through the homes of this indigenous population, we stumbled suddenly one day into an unwanted act of voyeurism. Apparently, the dung beetles and inchworms agreed that this particular morning was a fine day to begin the mating season. The first dung beetle I saw was all alone. I had never seen one in the wild, I watched enthralled while it roll its ball around the trail.

Over the course of the next few hours, that novelty would wear off pretty quickly as the sounds of thousands of dung beetles mating would make the forest practically sing with primal delight.

Everywhere we looked, everywhere we stepped: dung beetles.

And to make any insectophobe feel all the more uncomfortable, a glance up from the ground would reveal that the air was filled with small, floating inchworms dangling by their strings. It became impossible to walk without being covered in them. No longer was the crawling sensation on your neck just a mosquito, but perhaps an inchworm; one could only be certain after the latter made a far gooier squish when smashed against the base of the skull, into hair, or onto the clothes.

But as quickly as it had begun, just a day or two later, it was over; and we were glad of it.

∙ ∙ ∙

During this section in the middle of Virginia, we were joined for a few days by both John and Platypus. This was a nice bit of socialization to mix up our quiet days together. They also helped keep the mood light as the green tunnel of the longest state threatened to become oppressive.

One of our first days walking together, Platypus received the shocking news that I had never before seen "Rent" the musical, and he pledged to tell the whole story the next day. To the amazement of our entire group, he went above and beyond; not only did he tell the story start to finish, but he sang all the songs as well. I felt like I was right there on Broadway without ever leaving the woods.

We were all so impressed by his effort that we each took a day ourselves, doing the best we could to match his enthusiasm as we told our own stories. While Chilly also has a beautiful singing voice and treated us to her rendition of "The Sound of Music", John and I struggled to maintain the same quality of delivery in our own renditions; even so, being involved in such entertainment like the bards of the Middle Ages was an experience I won't soon forget.

One of the best known national parks in this area of Virginia is the Shenandoah. Before I started the trail, my brother and I decided he would join me for the Smokies section of my trip; but due to circumstances outside his control, we later changed our shared section to the Shenandoahs instead. Having separated from Platypus and John the day before, Chilly and I walked into the park by way of Skyline Drive, a scenic highway that tours through the one hundred plus miles of this park and provides numerous places where cars can pull over to enjoy glorious outlooks.

My parents dropped my brother off at one of these outlooks, then joined us themselves for a short day-hike. We were just heading into summer, but the air rippled with heat waves. The outing was particularly hard on my mom who, while in decent physical shape, had not hiked a trail this steep in some time. I think that day stimulated her back into a workout routine that included daily treadmill walking, definitely a healthy practice. At the top of this mountain we reached a bald summit where large boulders were strewn across several hundreds of feet in a fashion that looked almost as if they were arranged into a flattened pyramid. We took to boulder hopping to reach the peak on this otherwise bald face. It was good to hike with my parents like this, and we would see them again at the end of the Shenandoahs; but for now, my parents would return down to the car and my brother and I, along with Chilly, would continue on our way.

My brother, for his part, came much better prepared for this trip than for our last. He had replaced his external frame hand-me-down with a new Osprey, and the old unpackable sleeping bag rated at -20° with a much more reasonable 20° down bag. No longer considered state of the art, the tent he carried was my old reliable Clip Flashlight 2 by Sierra Designs – still one of my favorite designs on the market.

He still recounts how much he enjoyed that four day-hike in the Shenandoahs; but how could you not with beautiful views spaced periodically the length of the park, and being involved with the northbound thru-hiker bubble is an experience unlike any other. All of us were additionally quite fond of the wayside buildings which offered lunch, ice cream, and beer.

That being said, I believe my brother learned another valuable lesson (much like his first time on the AT). This time it had to do with chafing, and the urgency with which one must deal with hot spots before they become a bloody mess. To those of you reading this, take the message to heart: hot spots and chaffing require immediate attention. The most critical issues usually involved salt build up on hot days. This will then be rubbed into sensitive areas of skin leaving extremely painful rashes. Hot spots on the foot are far more favorable, and can usually be fixed with tape (Leukotape being by far the best option in my opinion) and possibly a better sock and shoe combination like the toe socks I had been wearing since North Carolina.

The other thru-hikers were eager (or perhaps overeager) to share with my brother their (sometimes new-found) knowledge, even though some of them had never experienced overnight backpacking prior to the Appalachian Trail. My brother had done at least some backpacking over the years since our first trip, so this sometimes rubbed him the wrong way. Completely understandable. But by this time, even the greenhorns had their trail legs and were starting to see themselves as something akin to experts in their field.

After a few days together with my brother, our parents picked us up near the end of the Shenandoah National Park and took us back to a campground where they had left their camper. We were able to get showers and do our laundry there. We pitched our tent at their campsite for the night too, and were treated to hamburgers and picnic foods – a refreshing break from the backpacking food which was becoming so repetitive and unexciting.

It was also at this campsite that I learned about a death that both saddened and angered me. Before I started my thru-hike, I had left a relationship of several years. Because of the seriousness of this relationship, I had very nearly pledged to become a custodian of my partner's niece in the event of the parent's death. This very narrowly failed to materialize, and I ended our relationship prior to leaving for the trail.

The child's mother had been clean for several years, but ended up overdosing soon after meeting her new boyfriend. At once sad over the death, and for the child, but angry that the death was preventable and took place in front of the child. At the same time, I felt as though I had narrowly dodged a bullet. Had the dice fallen differently, I may have been forced to leave both the trail and Chilly.

It was a lot to bear.

I walked to the bathroom block to take a hot shower and collect myself away from my new partner to prevent the risk of scaring her away at the sight of it. I left that shower absolved once more from burdens of the past, and a renewed appreciation of the freedom provided by my escape to the woods.

Later on the trail, when I was ready, I would share this experience with Chilly. She would listen and console me, much like we did for each other through the sickness, and much like we would do for each other in the trials ahead.

As with life off the trail, this is what both tests and strengthens a partnership – the trials requiring trust and reliability of someone else's support. With Chilly and I, it was unshakable.

These factors made hiking with a significant other so much better than doing it solo, or even with a friend. The trail consists of countless ups and downs; I'm sharing some of them here, but I shared all of them with her.

Some hiking partners, or even tramilies, will simply keep walking if someone has a hard day or struggles to keep up. But Chilly and I knew we could count on each other, knew that neither would let the other give up, nor let the other grow lonely. I set out on the trail with a high confidence that I would finish the thru-hike, but finding Chilly would all but guarantee it. Nothing would split us up.

• • •

After my parents took us back to the trail, Chilly and I set off again on our own. We only made it a couple miles before the wind picked up and the sky got dark. The race was on as we frantically searched for a flat piece of ground on which to pitch the tent. Just as we were throwing the last of our gear inside, the rain began coming in sheets; a flash storm that would have threatened to flood us out had we not been on the ridge line.

Our tent rattled, and the rain pelted us relentlessly. Huddled together in safety, we saw from beneath the rainfly a set of five feet walking by with a rapidity which we found this tent space just moments ago. Familiar voices brought complaints about the sudden shift in weather, but the Corey family continued to push through the storm. Those must be some of the toughest kids I've ever met.

The end of Virginia was almost in sight. Within a day or two we came to a giant mile marker made of stones.

"1000"

Now that's one hell of a journey! Almost half way, but nowhere near ready to stop.

Our last major challenge in this state was a 13 mile section called the Virginia Roller Coaster which ended at the West Virginia border. Although the peaks were not terribly high, the landscape's oscillations were frequent and steep with many rocks and loose rubble on which to lose your footing. The day we finished the roller coaster is the first day I can remember being grumpy towards the trail itself. I dripped with sweat, tired and worn out with all the ups and downs, and the mosquitoes were just starting to mount their summer offensive. I got into such a huff, and started hiking with such speed, that I stormed right past the sign for the border.

Chilly yelled ahead to me, "Welcome to West Virginia!"

This meant the end of the coaster and the approach to Harpers Ferry along with the halfway point of the AT. All of this lightened my mood considerably as we left behind the trail's longest state.

Other stories from the AT may give the impression that Virginia is somehow boring. This negative impression of Virginia has less to do with the natural beauty and more to do with it being by far the longest state, by mileage, on the trail. Couple that with its positioning about a month into the thru-hike when people are starting to find the trail less novel, and it results in what we call the death of the honeymoon period, or the "Virginia Blues". Walking for days on end, the green tunnel has a way of wearing on the psyche in some; I believe this impacted me more than it affected Chilly. Even so, the major impact of walking in the green tunnel was yet to come.

However, I believe that Virginia's many sights, sprawling landscapes, and natural biodiversity provide many romantic opportunities that support the state motto "Virginia is for lovers". This balance of beauty and hardship is what thru-hiking is all about. Eventually, people either submit to the "Virginia Blues", or they learn how to do it for the love of hiking rather than the love of great views, waterfalls, or other grand destinations. It's a bit like learning the journey is more important than the goal, then putting that realization into practice. Days in the green tunnel also pit one against questions of pushing more miles to get through versus taking time to smell the roses.

Balancing all of these mental factors – that is the real challenge of the Appalachian Trail, and it's what successful thru-hiking requires.

RESOLVE, DASHED AGAINST THE ROCKS

> *"Everything can be taken from a man but one thing: the last of the human freedoms — to choose one's attitude in any given set of circumstances, to choose one's own way."* –Viktor E. Frankl

Harper's Ferry is the unofficial halfway point of the Appalachian Trail, a quaint little town with historic significance stemming from the Civil War. The trail skirts around the town for a bit before coming up near Storer College, a historically black college closed in 1955 but kept intact for historical purposes just like the town itself. We made our way through town to reach the Appalachian Trail Conservancy headquarters where we were able to sign the registry and have our halfway photo taken for their records. This headquarters is an interesting place in its own right, containing a lounge specifically for thru-hikers to relax, recharge, and eat ice cream. It also houses the largest 3D topographic map of the Appalachian Trail I've ever seen. I spent some time talking with one of the volunteers there, and enjoyed the camaraderie with others who had reached the midpoint.

Our plan for Harpers Ferry involved taking the train into town all the way to Washington DC where we would spend two nights exploring, letting Chilly experience our nation's capital, and visiting some of the best museums in the world. I'm always interested in a good museum, but the Smithsonian is an unparalleled institution and one of my favorite destinations in DC.

The train ride itself didn't take long, waiting for the train was longer. 45 minutes later we entered DC at Grand Central Station and walked to the REI to replace some worn gear. I was keen to replace my shoes for the second time on the trail after putting more than 600 miles on my second pair. I left REI with a fresh pair of Timp 1.5s and sent the old pair home to my parents (as I would do with each set of shoes). As a Christmas present that year, my parents would give me a giant photo collage from the trail. On the frame they hung the worn out shoes, along with my namesake hat which I had repaired numerous times during the thru-hike.

The Airbnb we rented was a newly converted apartment building, clean and recently updated. On our first full day in town, we caught an Uber down to the Lincoln Memorial where we would start our journey, spending some time here and at each memorial or monument on our way to the Congress building at the other end of the mall. We also walked through the natural history museum, the Holocaust museum, and the portrait gallery. This was a nice vacation from trail life, though we were certainly out of place in the museums and government building while wearing our hiking clothes (but what else were we to wear?).

John met up with us at the congress building. We had hoped to see the senate chambers; but as Americans, John and I would have had to visit our state senator's office to get tickets. When we mentioned that Chilly was a foreigner, however, they said "Oh, well in that case here is a ticket for her and two guest tickets for you".

Somehow, it's easier for foreigners to get into our government buildings than it is for American citizens! Consider me flabbergasted.

●●●

We enjoyed our stay in DC, but being away from the trail before completing the thru-hike felt a bit odd. Even though we counted this a zero day, we still walked plenty of off-trail miles and didn't get much rest.

This was a big mistake in retrospect!

Upon returning to Harper's Ferry by train, we stopped into an ice cream shop before setting off again. It's notable that while Harper's Ferry is right on the trail, there were no advertisements for hostels. As it turns out, the only one isn't on the trail at. Seems odd to have such a trail town but almost nowhere to stay for the hikers. This is actually due to the fact that Harpers Ferry is a historical site, and there are limitations to where such establishments can be placed. Thru-hikers should keep this in mind; and if you are in a bind, there is a small field just before town where we were able to stay a night before catching the train.

When leaving Harper's Ferry, hikers cross the train bridge where the rail heads underground. Hikers break off from the tracks and circumnavigate the mountain back into the woods. At just four miles long, West Virginia makes up the shortest section of the trail. Soon enough we were headed into Maryland.

That first night in Maryland we stayed at the Dahlgren Backpack Campsite. We ordered pizza from the nearby town. Apparently, this was common enough practice that the delivery guy knew right where we would be. That either happened to be one of the best pizzas I've ever had, or I was simply pizza deprived having not eaten any to this point on trail.

We had only one more day in Maryland, and then just like that, the state's 40 easy miles were behind us. Next up, one of the most dreaded states on the trail: Pennsylvania.

● ● ●

The Pennsylvania section of the Appalachian Trail is a thing of legend and horror for northbound thru-hikers, a source of apprehension since the beginning of the trail. Even if they had not heard the tales, rumor and gossip would soon have everyone dreading the inevitable experience that awaited us just past the halfway point of our journey.

The southern entrance to Pennsylvania can be deceptively easy for anyone expecting endless days of rocky trail; but this only makes the sudden appearance of difficult terrain that much more brutal when it finally happens. Upon leaving the small town of Palmerton Pennsylvania, we were faced with one of the best rock scrambles I have seen on this side of the Mississippi. It loomed large, a pyramid of rubble. If you ever see pictures from the AT, you may recognize this climb by the American flag spray painted on the rocks.

This is where the trail changes dramatically, a line in the sand, made of boulders and talus. While we would later find that the rocks in New Jersey and New York were every bit as common as those in Pennsylvania, these later rocks were mostly large boulders while Pennsylvania prefers to torture hikers with small, unstable, ankle-breakers.

Like other thru-hikers, I had heard the stories about Pennsylvania as early as day three on trail. I knew that the state had ended more than a few thru-hikes that were going well until this point. Horror stories such as these lead some to go as far as changing their shoes. It's not uncommon for hikers that were using trail runners to switch into boots, grasping at the illusion of increased ankle stability. This is the recipe for disaster. As NOBO thru-hikers, they would have spent over 1000 miles in something with completely different structure, support, and heel to toe drop angle. This change can lead to strains and sprains, as well as muscle pain that will last the entire state and end up being considerably worse than just sticking with shoes.

The real takeaway here is that you will need to become used to whatever shoe you pick, and once you start, it will likely take a few hundred miles to develop "trail legs". This is the point after which your muscles and conditioning are used to the trail.

The aches and pains, while omnipresent to some degree, will lessen greatly and become a minor annoyance as opposed to a risk of injury.

I told you that first so that you can take what I say next with a grain of salt: those damn rocks often got the better of my temper, and more than a few times led to a stubbed toe.

The irony was that Chilly, wearing sandals, had very little trouble with the rocks. Surprisingly, her sandals were able to absorb the shock and protect her toes better than a trail running shoe could. Although neither of us sprained our ankles or had other significant damage from the rocks, walking over them for miles on end can be mentally draining due to the amount of focus required. For endless miles the trail brings hikers over oddly angled rocks, some of which are unstable and threaten to toss hikers off the trail without any notice. This is made all the worse for those carrying large packs which sway back and forth – all of this demands far more shoe-gazing, and far less "smelling of the roses" than anyone expects. We had the benefit of doing it with small packs. I pity those who walk this section wearing their 40 pound pack like a giant tortoise shell.

●●●

Just past the official halfway point, we got off the trail for an overnight stay in Middlesex, PA. The green tunnel and the rocks were starting to fray our nerves. The soft warm bed and continental breakfast held the allure of a siren's song in vast, unforgiving sea.

We checked out of the hotel after our first night stay, made our way back down the highway, and found the trailhead. But we would not be hiking very far today.

For reasons that escape her even now, Chilly had one of her worst days on trail just one mile outside Middlesex. I had been walking ahead, as I sometimes did, when I suddenly realized she wasn't behind me any longer. Walking back down the trail, I found her sitting on a stump, looking shook up and exasperated. With no explanation, the will to walk any further left her.

We hadn't planned on taking a zero day here, but one was apparently necessary.

So we stood up together, and shambled back to town. Almost instantly, her mood improved and her sprits lifted. We checked back into the hotel, to the surprise of the front desk worker who recognized our distinctive smell I'm sure, and enjoyed the rest of the day with TV, oranges, and chocolates. She was a little upset that I wouldn't let her eat the random Ziploc bag of skittles from the hiker box, but she got over it.

That's how you pass the norovirus, guess she had forgotten Gatlinburg!

Our extra stay provided us the mental recharge we needed to make it through the rest of Pennsylvania. This was one of the very few actual zero days we took on the entire hike, and it was more than welcome.

• • •

We spend countless days walking over fields of rocks. Realistically, it probably wasn't all that long; but focusing on your foot placement for 10+ hours a day, in the summer heat, isn't what I would call "fun". No wonder people warned us about PA...

But eventually we were granted another moment of respite. While approaching the town of Warwick, we learned from our Guthook app (a GPS map and list of trail towns that proved invaluable on the AT) that the local drive-in theater allowed thru-hikers to camp onsite. Compared to the small drive-in theaters near my hometown, this place was massive. Three giant screens, each bigger than the last. Three separate double features playing simultaneously.

For a technology deprived hiker, it was magical. Plus, there was a hotdog stand!

The place was packed, and the thru-hikers were given a patch of grass on a hill at the back. I had a substantial walk down to retrieve my well-deserved hotdogs from the middle of the venue; but having walked from Georgia, I suppose saying so sounds a bit ridiculous. There must have been 15 to 20 thru-hikers there; and while we all kept to our own kind, the beer flowed and everyone had fun. We all needed something to think about other than the rocks.

But outdoor theaters don't plan their movie showings around the schedules of thru-hikers, and soon hiker midnight came and we couldn't keep our eyes open any longer. I fell asleep that night to the sound of Woody from Toy Story, excited at having just reunited with Little Bow Peep.

● ● ●

To complete a thru-hike of the Appalachian Trail requires overcoming many additional challenges most people probably never expect an outdoors adventure to entail. Increasingly obvious to us as we made our way north, cities in United States are becoming hostile to pedestrian traffic.

American towns, once designed for short distance travel, are losing their walkability. Chopped to pieces by highways and ever bigger roads, the sidewalk is becoming extinct even in places that otherwise cater to long distance hikers. Anything larger than a small trail town poses far more threat to a thru-hiker's wellbeing than any bear or snake in the forest, that's how I see it.

Pennsylvania just so happens to be the worst state for such dangers. The once sleepy German settlement of Hamburg, Pennsylvania is a prime example – but it's just one of many. Having always been a trail town, Hamburg is just a short walk south from where the AT skirts the city limits. Then the interstate was built, connecting Pennsylvania to New York City, and with it came ever increasing traffic. Next came the Walmart Supercenters, Lowe's, and everything else. In 2003, the international outdoor retail giant, Cabela's, decided to place its largest ever establishment here to take advantage of the high-traffic location.

Every road into town was now packed, what is a thru-hiker to do? Instead of risking our lives walking, we phoned the Cabela's on rumor they may provide a shuttle to the store. Sure enough, a people mover soon showed up to take us right to the front gate of this monument to capitalistic expansion.

We needed more bug repellent anyway; and who could resist checking this place out, if only for a minute?

The interior was practically a zoo, real animals in every direction we looked. Except, well, they were all stuffed. Not the fish of course. That display, with its thirty foot waterfall, was filled to the brim with colorful trout and other specimen – likely used to keep the children occupied while dad bought his new gun or fishing gear.

We were out of our element here, and it must have been obvious because a well-dressed man approached us asking what our story was. Upon telling him of our exploits, he just handed us some cash and wouldn't consider taking it back. He must have felt like he was contributing to a grand adventure; it made us feel like the drifters we obviously were.

Leaving there as soon as we got our repellant, the next challenge would be restocking at the local Walmart. From the parking lot of Cabela's, we saw Walmart almost close enough to hit with a thrown rock, yet separated from us by an impassable sea of fast-moving traffic. Returning to Cabela's to find an alternative path, we were informed by the front desk a short walk down a few side streets and under a bridge would deliver us to Walmart.

Nothing to it he said. Except the roads here don't have sidewalks...

We spent the next 45 minutes walking in road ditches and uneven shoulders, getting buzzed by oncoming cars several times a minute, and inhaling enough exhaust fumes to make an elephant dizzy. Upon finally reaching our destination, I felt more gritty and grimy that I did after a week in the woods without a shower. Worn out, and nerves frayed, we made quick work of our restocks just so we could leave this blemish of a city as soon as possible.

Not willing to risk our lives again on the return trip to Cabela's, we called an Uber driver who was not the least bit surprised that we need his help.

● ● ●

Pennsylvania refused to let us leave without throwing one more curveball at us. Ambling through an absolute obstacle course of a trail, as we had been for days, we stumbled upon a recent sign posted on a tree near a junction. This sign suggested we ought to take an alternate route due to a little flooding on the AT caused by beavers. Being unflappable trail purists, we scoffed at the idea of some beavers forcing us to skip white blazes. And so we took the official trail which abruptly dropped down from the ridgeline into the valley below.

It didn't take long before we realized this was no simple beaver family, but an entire beaver army who had commissioned a dam more than a mile long. The small amount of flooding we expected turned out to include thigh deep muck, but we trudged through anyway. Chilly, completely unphased in her sandals and shorts, led the way while I followed begrudgingly in shoes that soon had the drag weight of lead bricks. I didn't even get to see the beavers; lucky for them too, their manager was going to get a piece of my mind.

At least that's how I remembered it. Expert review of the video footage later revealed that the dam only took us three minutes to pass, far less than a mile, and the water only came to my shin...

This state was clearly causing me to blow small inconveniences out of proportion, I would need to be mindful to keep my sanity out here.

Soon enough we left the valley once more, heading to higher elevation and another mountain summit. Once on the other side, we were treated to another sweeping valley below and realized we had reached the Delaware Water Gap. This marked the line between Pennsylvania and New Jersey where a long bridge reaches across a winding river acting as the border between states. The approach to this bridge brings a bird's eye view of the river and border crossing several miles prior to setting foot on the bridge.

The river here brought my mind to the open plains of the western US, its meandering path through the valley reminiscent of Dead Horse Point in Utah. A peaceful scene, and welcome divergence from the green tunnel for thru-hikers heading northbound.

Upon entering town, we set our sights on the most important of trail necessities: ice cream. The little shop was close enough to trail that many packs were stacked out front by the time we arrived. Inside, we were greeted with a quaint 50's style ice cream bar. I ordered my standard root beer float and a large cherry sundae for us to split, then we went back for a plateful of hotdogs, and then an order of chocolates. Not to worry, the calories didn't stand a chance against our thru-hiker metabolism.

As we neared the end of our meal, a kindly older gentleman stood up from his table where he sat with his grandkids and walked our way. He could probably tell from our odd clothes, and the smell, that we were thru-hikers. If I didn't know better, I would have thought that it was *HIS* lucky day to have met *US*; but it was most certainly Chilly and I who were lucky.

Pete, as he had introduced himself, absolutely insisted on paying our bill in exchange for hearing a bit about our story. He was thrilled to hear that we had met on trail, and were getting pretty serious about it too.

"Invite me to your wedding someday," he said through the biggest smile I had seen from a non-hiker in months.

"And if you wait here 'til I drop off the grandkids, I will swing back 'round and take you up to the grocery store."

We agreed, and they left immediately. About ten minutes later, we were sitting on a bench outside when here comes Pete in a sharp white Camaro.

"Someone said you guys needed a lift!"

"Yeh, Pete, someone sure did!"

Thanks for your kindness that day Pete. You will be hearing from us soon, as requested.

CITY SKYLINES AND ROCKY ESCARPMENTS

"All my adult life I have been a guest in other people's houses, following the sun and seasons like a migratory bird, an instinct in me." –Stanley Elkin

New York State was a real change of pace from the green tunnel of the south; its expanded landscapes and diverse color palette but a suggestion of what would come as we continued north. We spent many miles clambering over boulders at the edge of an escarpment, views and long drop-offs a plenty. Although these high ridgelines were essentially devoid of biting bugs, dropping down to the valleys almost guaranteed being swarmed with mosquitoes. We soon came to disdain the downhills which led back into mosquito territory, nearly sprinting through these sections just to reach the next mountain. Upon heading uphill we would rejoice, for high elevation promised a momentary respite from the bugs of the dense forest below.

After our escape to Washington DC, we were quite excited to do the same when we reached New York City. Our plan to get from the trail to the city was to catch a commuter bus that left from Bear Mountain Inn. Before we approached the inn, we came to a mountain peak which gave us our first view of New York City from approximately 50 miles away. After spending a few months in the woods with only short stops in the various towns along the way, this view of the city scape from the distance, set against the ocean backdrop, was breathtaking. I have always felt an attraction to city sky lines, but had never observed one from an obscure mountain peak at a distance such as this.

Like stepping out of the primitive old world and into the new, it was complete with enough neon brilliance and noise to make our heads spin. Even compared to DC, New York City is completely a world apart from the trail we had just left.

We caught an Uber from the Port Authority Bus Terminal to Lower Manhattan where we would be staying once again in a renovated apartment building. I make that trip sound much simpler than it actually was; but in reality, we were treated (against our will, due to driver error) to a tour of Lower Manhattan by car. Although the ride was interesting in its own right, it took up almost two hours of our day. Thankfully, Uber refunded the trip and spared us the $200 that had been accumulated.

Our exploration of Manhattan by foot took us to Battery Park, from which we could see the Statue of Liberty, to Wall Street and Time Square. Time Square was particularly overwhelming with its larger than life screens and advertisements, those neon gods, which stood in stark contrast to both the green tunnel and the relative isolation provided by the trail. Long gone were the bird sounds and wind whipping through trees, replaced by honking cars and commuters living their lives.

As such, we needed a little trail to go with our city. Based on a recommendation from a fellow thru-hiker, we sought out the High Line. This raised walkway had been converted from an old railway and was now filled with greenery and provided a bird's eye view of the streets below.

Later, when searching for a restroom in the cement jungle, we stumbled into the Chelsea Markets which were like an industrial underground with eateries and shops offering many sorts of things which are generally of little value during a thru-hike. Though it was a different kind altogether, we very much enjoyed our adventure through town that day.

That evening we had tickets to see a Broadway show: The Book of Mormon. We showed up wearing what we always wore, and while we felt just a little out of place at first, I suppose very little in the way of dress strikes a New Yorker as odd. The show was absolutely hilarious, and I would highly recommend it to anyone who doesn't mind a little sacrilege along with their belly-laughing.

• • •

Returning to Bear Mountain from New York City we headed off toward the zoo. I suppose you didn't know there was a zoo right on the AT did you?

It's spoken of like it's a great idea; but for a thru-hiker trying to walk every mile of the trail, to see every white blaze, and to follow the guidelines of the 2000-Miler Club – its's absolutely appalling. Whoever came up with this idea should be publicly shamed. You see, unlike long-distance hiking trails, zoos have business hours; and we just happened to miss them. Upon seeing this, I was livid. Not only did they put a gate right in the middle of the AT, they forced us to walk out and around on a blue blazed trail just to meet up on the other side!

I was having none of it. The front gate was too big, and too obvious, to climb; so I did what they wanted and stomped my way around on the alternate path. Upon arriving at the back gate, I found it unlocked. This made my job much easier, as I would have gotten in either way.

That day I technically broke into the zoo, and did my first southbound mile on the Appalachian Trail; and it felt damn good too, right up until the security guard found me giving an angry rant about the whole thing into my phone's video recorder. Our interaction was a mix of him being understanding, and me being utterly impossible to convince; so he escorted me on my way south and let me out the gate.

In my victory, I didn't even mind having to re-walk the alternate trail back around!

After this little escapade, we strolled across a bridge spanning the Hudson River and heading back into the woods. Being out of the city, and off the roadway, provided an immediate sense of relief. Life slowed from a sprint to a saunter once more.

Soon after leaving town, Chilly and I began making plans for when we might finish the trail. There was no reason to do so this early on the trail, other than the fact that we had received a wedding invitation. The date of the wedding was sometime near our expected end date. In order to make it on time, we needed to increase our average miles per day quite a bit. Not an unreasonable amount, but not insignificant.

No sooner than we had made these plans, the trail reminded us that hopes and dreams don't by themselves make a thru-hike successful. You have to put in the work. We still think to this day that the planning itself is part of what made it less enjoyable for those couple of weeks. Up to that point, we had only planned from one restock to the next for almost the entire trail. This was a level of freedom which made the trail more manageable. Now, we were looking far ahead, estimating how hard this climb, or that section might be.

As you might have guessed, after a week or two of this we gave up on racing to the finish and went back to winging it. Realizing we couldn't comfortably make it on time allowed us to ease up on the miles and take more time to relax on mountaintops, or take naps lying beside the dazzling beaches which dot the northern woods.

I'm sorry to have missed the wedding, but deciding not to push ourselves was a huge stress relief and just what we needed at the time.

● ● ●

With Chilly's 30th birthday coming up, I had tried to find some type of cake or pastry for her. Unfortunately, our restock just before the date turned out to be little more than a gas station convenience store. Not very convenient if you ask me.

And so, I settled on fudge rounds...

Turns out, she doesn't even like fudge rounds. That wouldn't have been so bad if we didn't also spend most of her birthday hiding from the heavy rain in a shelter that was filled with mosquitoes.

She took it well, but it wasn't the best birthday I'm sure. I tried to lift the mood by telling her what my dad had told me over the phone on my birthday:

"You are doing exactly what you wanted to do this summer, and you're doing it very well!"

Sometimes it's hard to enjoy the trail in the moment, that type 2 fun; but this is what we signed up for after all.

About two weeks later, a birthday package from her family arrived. Having come from New Zealand, it was held up in customs longer than expected and needed to be shipped ahead to our location on the trail. That evening we had real, homemade cake from her mum while we watched a video they had sent showing them singing happy birthday to a cardboard cutout with her face on it.

Chilly shed tears of joy. She had been away from her family, and in a foreign country, for three and a half months by this point. This present was worth more than all the cake and candies they could have fit in a gift box.

And certainly more than that fudge round I'd given her.

● ● ●

Near the end of New York State, the trail drops down to a large lake and heads around a little peninsula to a large, open beach. This is Clarence Fahnestock State Park, complete with free showers and a snack bar where we were able to purchase some hotdogs.

You may be noticing a trend: if there are hotdogs, I'm all over them. It's odd, actually. I never much cared for hotdogs before the trail, they kind of disgusted me honestly. But tastes change dramatically when you spend that long in the woods, and hotdogs certainly weren't the strangest thing I had eaten on this trip. That distinction almost certainly belonged to the peanut butter and tuna tortillas.

My eyes closed in ecstasy, savoring the hot, processed, meat-equivalent of junk food that made up my lunch as the storm started rolling in. Closing time was also approaching, and the workers were starting to lock up the buildings and restrooms. These restrooms were family sized and included showers and benches. All things considered, they were extremely clean. We decided rather than hike several miles to the next shelter, we would just ask the employee to leave one of the bathrooms unlocked so that we could shelter there instead. He agreed, likely breaking protocol, and looked the other way while we began setting up our home for the night.

Using rocks from their landscaping instead of tent stakes, we pitched the bug net inside the bathroom to provide a clean, waterproof area in which we could keep our stuff. Other than that, camp was as normal as ever. Sure, it was probably the most hiker-trash thing we had ever done; but we were warm and dry that night while the storm raged outside.

Thru-hiking: the adventure where you pay thousands of dollars to live in voluntary homelessness.

We rose early the next morning and scampered off into the woods before too many people noticed what we had done. Soon we would be out of the state and making our way into Connecticut. Here the trail quickly cuts through the northwest corner of the state and heads into Massachusetts; with just 52 miles of Connecticut, we did it with just one overnight stay. On the evening of the next day we walked into Massachusetts with Connecticut little more than a blip on the radar.

Southern Massachusetts continues the relatively flat profile we had become accustomed to since the Shenandoahs of Virginia, its first few mountains not raising above 3000 feet. It's also home to Mt. Greylock, a name befitting the mysterious and misty mountain covered in a tall, thick pine grove. We walked a path woven through pines, switchback after switchback, heading up into the space where clouds slither between trees in the early morning. Near the flat, spacious summit we took a small detour deeper into the pines before bursting suddenly into a clearing where a shelter sat, overrun with a group of hikers who had already gathered for lunch. The ascent up this mountain was the most elevation we had climbed in hundreds of miles, it heralded the steep climbs that would mark the northern Appalachian range.

FORTITUDE TESTED IN THE SWAMPS OF VERMONT

"Walk so that your footprints bear only the mark of peaceful joy and complete freedom. To do this, you have to learn to let go. Let go of your sorrows, let go of your worries. This is the secret of walking meditation." –Thich Nhat Hanh

The trail in these two small states was a nice break from the rocks and boulder hopping of Pennsylvania and New York. Those few hundred miles were mild and allowed us to recover somewhat before our final set of challenges which would begin once we set foot in Vermont.

The Appalachian Trail follows the Vermont Long Trail for some one hundred miles, and is home to the beautiful Green Mountain Range. Vermont is also known for its bog bridges, muddy terrain, and mosquito infested cesspools, especially after the AT leaves the Long Trail at a place called "Maine Junction".

Starting at the border between Massachusetts and Vermont, the Long Trail predates the Appalachian Trail itself. Here we traversed endless rolling emerald mountains and were treated to numerous vistas; however, the experience was primarily marked by sweat, struggle, and bugs. The heat of the summer led to an endless cycle of sweating out my electrolytes, then struggling to replace them with various drink mixes and multivitamins. In addition, we were constantly covered in toxic DEET in a futile effort to combat the swarms of bugs that grew from a minor nuisance into the trail's greatest mental challenge to date.

Acting as a sweatband around my head, my buff had become saturated with a disgusting amalgamation of chemicals and salty grime. One day in the Green Mountains, we sat down by a small stream trickling gently from the steep slopes. In this quiet and peacefully respite, I removed the buff and gently wiped the sweat from around my eyes.

Just seconds later I realized the magnitude of my mistake to the tune of searing agony and my own subsequent cursing. The calm was broken, panic ensued!

Between the DEET and the concentrated salts, I couldn't open my eyes!

I called out desperately for help. Chilly ran over to find me clutching my face in my hands. She rushed to rinse the buff in the stream before applying it to my eyes. This was probably not the most ecologically friendly approach given its toxicity, but I certainly wasn't complaining (at least not about ecology). Once again, I didn't know what I would do without her. I might have been left stumbling around blind!

These hardships are simply part and parcel of thru-hiking. Doing our best to fight through them, we took solace in the approaching end to the green tunnel, and the ever taller mountains as we marched north. The mountains were returning, we were leaving the valleys behind.

Perhaps the best example of this forest's inspirational beauty is Stratton Mountain, the mountain from which Benton McKay first envisioned the linking of the Whites, the Greens, and mountains of the south into a single trail. From the fire tower, we could see his vision before us, where we had been and what was yet to come.

Who could stand here and not be driven to wander from this mountain range to those distant peaks in the northeast?

• • •

The rough times of Vermont continued as we left the Green Mountain range and dropped down into the low elevation swamps in the eastern part of the state. It was miserable.

Well into summer now, the heat and bugs were reaching their zenith. We spent days on end draining bottles of bug spray onto our skin and clothes, flailing impotently against the hordes of mosquitoes – each a potential carrier for a litany of deadly diseases. Not to mention the ceaseless itching that came with it, or the neurotic slapping and paranoia at every tickle or movement of hair in the breeze. If it wasn't the mosquitoes, it was the flies which infested our heads like moles burrowing into their new home, or the gnats whose suicidal quest for moisture led many to their death inside my ocular cavity and resulted in temporary, but periodic, blindness. In New York these had been simple pests, but now they had amassed into an onslaught that would threaten to overwhelm us.

Most people who venture into the woods fear bears and snakes. Not me. The biologist in me panics at the thought of blood borne diseases and parasites passed on by biting insects. Chilly, on the other hand, doesn't know any better after having lived her whole life where such things don't exist. Maybe she's lucky.

I ask myself even now if the bugs were really that bad, or if my tolerance of them was simply evaporating. Either is possible; but, it was around this point when the daily walking combined with my day dreams of post-trail plans were all starting to wear me down. I expect the people who never feel like this on a thru-hike are both incredibly rare and practically super human. That being said, I don't think that Chilly ever felt quite as tormented as I did in this section of the trail.

"Eh, guess I can just blame it on the bugs."

The thought scuttled from my mind as I suddenly shot myself in the eye with bug spray, narrowly missing the backside of my arm. The feeling of poison meeting carefully balanced ocular juices tingled, quite unpleasantly, through my face.

To my chagrin, all the effort and bug repellants barely even slowed them down. I had seen ticks crawling on freshly treated tights, and mosquitoes which would bite straight through them or find that single square inch you had missed with the spray. I had begun to lose faith in both DEET bug spray and permethrin treatment of my clothes. Leading up to this point I had been so careful, so paranoid about preventing tick borne disease; but it would all come to a head one morning in these swamps of Vermont.

I had slept well the night before; naked as usual, to keep my sleeping bag clean. My morning routine was the same as any other day: pull on the still moist tights and shirt, slip the shorts on while deflating my sleeping pad, and eat my pop tarts in the tent while Chilly scowled at me for inevitably making a mess with the crumbs. We got our camp packed up, and Chilly set off down the trail after telling her I needed a minute to "water" a nearby tree.

And there it was, the object of my paranoia, the harbinger of doom itself; like a carefree hiker strolling through the woods, a small black tick waddled its way from the tip of my manhood toward my hand. I stood aghast, fully immersed in a single, sparkling moment of fear which crystallized as I realized this was no dream, but nightmare manifest as reality, coalescing finally into a cool, calm rationalization:

There was a tick on my dick.

In a flash, countless session's worth of exposure therapy shoved down my throat, forcing me to face my fear. In that moment of clarity, I flicked the little miscreant from its perch and finished my business.

"Not today you little bastard."

I walked away from that encounter like a conqueror of some great feat, nearly skipping up the trail to find Chilly.

"You'll never guess what just happened!"

●●●

"Man does not simply exist but always decides what his existence will be, what he will become the next moment. By the same token, every human being has the freedom to change at any instant." –Viktor Emil Frankl, Man's Search for Meaning

●●●

Exiting the woods, we were able to catch a hitch with a hippie chick in a Jeep heading into the town of Rutland. A "farmer" at one of the organic places nearby, or so she claimed. When I probed a little further, she suggested tomatoes were her product of choice – I was less than convinced.

She dropped us off near a famed restaurant and hostel called the Yellow Deli. We didn't know it at the time, but we were walking into an establishment owned and operated by the Twelve Tribes, a religious organization many characterize as a cult. However, all we experienced was their kindness (and their amazing food).

Upon arrival, we were given a free helping of their special tea: yerba mate. They claim this tea has stimulating qualities that rival coffee, and the members of this organization drink it like camels at a desert oasis. Apparently the Twelve Tribes own massive farms in South America where they grow the stuff. It was OK, but I don't think I'll be switching form tea any time soon.

After we had checked in, they led us upstairs to the hiker hostel and informed us that men and women would be required to sleep in completely separate spaces. The women had the entire third floor to themselves. Additionally, all guests were expected to change from their hiking clothes into modest, plainly colored trousers and long shirts; women were given equally drab dresses.

We mustn't be tempted by colorful clothing or shared spaces...

Once we had changed and sorted out our gear, Chilly and I reunited down in the restaurant for dinner. Although we ordered seemingly simple sandwiches, they were easily among the best food we had on trail. I can't really explain why, must have been the special sauce.

The next morning we were all invited to a family style breakfast. One of the female thru-hikers had apparently missed the memo about avoiding the opposite sex. She had been caught sleeping in one of the men's beds the night before, and they were both asked to help with the breakfast as a form of penitence. Again, the food was amazing. They even sent us on our way with oranges for the trail ahead.

To get back on our journey, caught a bus to the trail head from which we had hitched the night before. At least, that's what we thought we were doing.

As it turned out, we ended up on the wrong bus despite confirming multiple times with bus attendants. Instead, we would be left at a trailhead eighteen miles north of our previous position. Being the fastidious white blazers we were, we decided to have a true SOBO day to finish those missed miles. This would also result in needing a hitch back to Rutland and the Yellow Deli that evening. It seemed to us the cult would not let us go after all, and the irony was not lost on anyone.

Our SOBO hike that day was an enjoyable change of pace and led us to seeing other NOBOs we had met previously. We were always quick to point out that they must be heading the wrong way, or that we just couldn't stay away from the Yellow Deli so we were heading back. In the end, we did just that.

The next morning we caught the same bus as the day before and we were back on our way north toward the end of the Vermont Long Trail.

● ● ●

At the end of our journey on Vermont's Long Trail we summited Killington Peak, home of what looked to be a very impressive ski field complete with distant views over steep drops into the valley below. Eventually, we found our path down from the mountain and into Killington city proper for a restock.

The trail from here beelines straight for the border with New Hampshire. Just outside of the Green Mountain range, we had our final run-in with the Corey family. We shared a swimming hole under a bridge with them, just a small patch of paradise from which we escaped the summer heat for a while.

After lunch, we took off on our own. However, it wasn't long before the kids caught up and wanted to hike with us a bit more. They were very excited to nearly be back to the White Mountains where they had trained before starting the AT proper. Chilly and I were as impressed as ever with their excitement and wherewithal even this late in the trail, it certainly rivaled my own! At one point we ran into some southbound thru-hikers who had heard of the family and assumed we were the parents!

We all had a laugh, but didn't stop to correct them; they were partially right about our group being family after all.

That afternoon, after we had bid the Corey kids farewell, we ran into Kentucky and Jeff once more. Like the Corey's, we had been seeing these two off and on for several states. Our experience with friends on the trail always took this pattern: meeting up after what felt like an eternity, reminiscing like old pals and catching up with the latest accomplishments. A game of leap frog all the way to Katahdin.

They decided to press onward when we stopped for the night

at Lookout Shelter. Perched on a bald overlook, this four sided cabin was so named because of a rooftop platform which could be reached by ladder. From that vantage point, we enjoyed a brilliant sunset before the evening chill chased us back inside. Although it looked like a house from the outside, the sleeping arrangements were nothing more than a wood plank floor where everyone spaced themselves out and set up their sleeping bags.

A group of overnight campers, college or high school age I suppose, decided to sleep up in the lookout itself. I'm not sure how they pulled it off, but somehow they fit four people in a space where I wouldn't be comfortable sleeping by myself. Maybe that means I'm losing the courage of youth...

On our way out of the state, we would find ourselves passing through a little pit stop of a town called West Hartford – the most notable feature being the bridge over which the trail crosses before passing a hostel where we would spend the night. A bridge of some renown among thru-hikers, this was known as the place from which you can jump 30 feet or more down to the river. Once we dropped off our gear in the old barn we would call home that evening, we donned swimming clothes (my laundry shorts, Chilly went in her underwear) and headed back to the bridge.

Although Chilly didn't want to jump, I headed straight for the guardrail. She decided to sit in the water below and film my escapades. I wasn't alone up there, several other thru-hikers had already jumped over the guardrail and stood on a ledge waiting their next turn. A little boy, maybe ten, waited his turn while receiving encouragement from his dad. It was his first time too.

I cautiously stepped, one foot at a time, over the railing. Edging closer, apprehensive, and making small talk with the father to help boost my own confidence.

Working up the courage took me longer than expected, and

maybe it didn't help that the boy decided he would try on another day; but after 15 minutes or so, I finally signaled to Chilly my readiness, and took the plunge.

Some might wonder what in the world I was thinking going out to the woods for nearly half a year, and others may think me crazy to jump from a bridge in a place I had never been; but events like free falling from such a height into an unknown river has a way of tapping into true joy, and the trail was full of moments just like this. The hardships wash away in an instant, flooded out by feelings of euphoria.

This is why we hike.

WHOSE IDEA WAS THIS ANYWAY?

> *"Walking the entire Appalachian Trail is not recreation. It is an education and a job...It is a challenging task – a journey with deeper ramifications."* –Warren Doyle

Somewhere around Pennsylvania, or Rocksylvania as it's often called, many thru-hikers probably ask the question, "What made me think I wanted to do this?"

If not there, then perhaps the swamps of Vermont would do it.

I'm sure this also crossed the minds of the Appalachian Trail legends too; but like those first trail blazers, most thru-hikers who have made it this far will find it in themselves to push forward. Having survived the difficulties of a long hike is a major contributing factor to the satisfaction of having completed it, after all.

When first conceived, no one expected that the Appalachian Trail would be walked end to end. That was simply not its purpose at the time. Instead, the mastermind behind it all, Benton MacKaye, imagined this long trail as a series of short distance connections between towns and farmsteads that would help revitalize a way of life lost to industrialization. In his almost utopian view, all who lived and worked along the length of the trail would contribute to the community and its shared interest. A century later, technology has outpaced MacKaye's practical plan but his philosophy is alive and well in the community, hiking clubs, and trail towns that give the AT a life of its own and draws people from the world over to saunter through its mountains.

The first AT thru-hiker, Earl Shaffer, walked the trail more than 20 years after it was first conceived. He did so at a time when the enthusiasm for such a project was dwindling; but, when news of his conquest started to spread, the trail found a new life and higher levels of support than ever. Having just returned home from WWII, Shaffer walked into the mountains to outpace his memories of war. In doing so, he served his country yet again by becoming a hero to many, and a spokesperson at the Appalachian Trail Conference where funding for the trail was successfully secured to keep MacKaye's dream alive.

Just seven years after Shaffer finished the first thru-hike, another legend would walk out of her front door after telling her family she was going on a walk. Grandma Gatewood, at 67 years old, would be the first woman to solo hike the entire AT. Moreover, having the impression from the news that the walk would be easy, and expecting clean shelters at the end of each day, she took little more than rain gear and a blanket. This would be the pioneering hike for what would later be called ultralight backpacking.

These trailblazers walked the AT for some of the same reasons people are still doing so today: escapism, enjoying nature, or even just for a "lark" as Gatewood has said. Today, the same reasons exist, but I tend to categorize thru-hikers' purpose for thru-hiking into just a few larger categories:

> 1. The Naturalist: people who hike to see the natural beauty of the trail, to take in the scenery and enjoy the fresh air.
>
> 2. The Challenge Seeker: the athletic hikers, the ones who do it because it's there, those who do it with gear restrictions/limitations, and those who have set it as a lifetime goal.
>
> 3. The Escapist: those who want to get away from it all

for a while, who need to find themselves, find God, or work out other personal or relationship problems.

I'm sure someone reading this will think of some reason to thru-hike that doesn't fit into these categories, but my experience with the trail and the community that surrounds it suggests these three will encompass most thru-hikers. I fit primarily into category #2, though like most, I also have significant interest in category #1. I might even argue that my goals to meditate as I walked and my minimalist approach after starting the trail helps me also makes me fit into category #3. I elaborate on this to make a point, a person's reasons for attempting a thru-hike are rarely simple and are often quite hard to explain with any certainty. AWOL addresses this as well:

"None of my peers could concisely articulate why they were doing a thru-hike. Most were motivated by a convergence of reasons. The time was right, they liked being outdoors, they were tired of their job (or their employer was tired of them), they wanted to lose weight, they had friends hiking, or they were inspired by another person's thru-hiking experience." -David "AWOL" Miller

It's almost comical when you compare the real reasons people thru-hike with the reasons normal people imagine. The common off-hand remark is something like, "Oh, is he hiking to find himself?"

Sure, many people are out there to do just that, or some iteration of it. Even one of the AMC campsite workers, who will remain anonymous, said to Chilly and me, "Everyone out here has some kind of problem they're working through".

That's clearly wrong, but this sentiment pervades the perceptions of thru-hiking to such a degree that everyone is colored in this light.

"Why do they always make movies about people with (messed) up lives, why can't thru-hikers have a movie about someone who finishes," a disgruntled thru-hiker said to me one day after hearing these sentiments one too many times.

The story of "Wild" becoming so popular may have something to do with that. The reality is that many people are just out for the challenge, adventure, natural beauty, or minimalist lifestyle provided by thru-hiking. In Appendix B, prospective thru-hikers will find several specific questions they can ask of themselves when thinking about their own reasons. This is but one critical form of preparation an aspiring thru-hiker should make before hitting the trailhead; because without clear purpose, few will find their way to the finish.

Anyone, hiker or otherwise, should know a certain number of things about themselves less they risk bumbling their way through life none the wiser. What will you do when shit hits the fan? How will you react to the difficult times that we must all inevitably face? What limits do you have on any number of things, and will you ever do anything that will put these limits to the test?

Whenever people ask about the purpose of a thru-hike, I always wonder what they think is the purpose of life itself.

As Americans, we're constantly being told that we live in the freest country on Earth; but most are latched onto paychecks and jobs like babies to the teat. Is that how people are supposed to live?

We have these spaces, public lands, and national resources where anyone can go to be just about as free as anyone could be on this Earth. Therefore, there will be as many reasons for using that freedom as there are people who seek it. The final leg of our journey made it clear, if there was ever an ounce of doubt before, the reasons why we hike and the beauty waiting for those with the gumption to go find it.

● ● ●

"No amount of security is worth the suffering of a mediocre life chained to a routine that has killed your dreams" –Maya Mendoza

ALPINE WONDERLAND

"It's not the mountain we conquer, but ourselves." –Sir Edmund Hillary

Leaving Vermont and entering New Hampshire, we were finally and completely ejected out of the green tunnel, thrust into the northern wilderness and abundant alpine ridgelines. The trail would progressively provide us with better views, harder climbs, and some of the best shelters and hostels on the entire trail.

At the summit of Smarts Mountain we found the first of such shelters. Both a fire warden's cabin and a fire tower had been built here, and subsequently abandoned, years prior. The warden's cabin was a four-sided stronghold located in just the right place to help us avoid the evening's storm. Ten of us all huddled together inside as the wind whipped up and the rain blew in. One brave hammock camper was nearly blown from his bed before he decided tonight was not a hammock night, and rushed in to join us. Everyone had a good laugh, and surely felt lucky to have such great home for the evening as the deluge made its presence known on the roof.

We almost always slept in our tent; but nothing is quite as soothing as falling asleep to the sound of rain on a shelter roof.

Several days later we came down from the mountains and entered the sleepy hamlet of Glencliff to stay at the Hikers Welcome Hostel. That night was movie night, though I think every night is movie night here. The trail hardened NOBOs huddled around a table eating popcorn and microwave pizzas. A true hiker's feast.

Just before the storm hit again that night, I enjoyed an outdoor shower and did a load of laundry. I wanted to completely recharge as we neared the famed mountain range of New Hampshire.

• • •

I was nearly giddy looking forward to the White Mountains, and I could almost taste victory waiting at the finish line. Caught up thinking about how great this section might be, and the challenges we would soon face, I almost missed the start of it. We climbed to the peak of Mount Moosilauke before realizing, with pleasant surprise, that we were already there. There was no question that the northernmost quarter of the trail would be like nothing we had experienced in the south. The Whites are widely renowned as the best section of the trail for good reason.

Our climb up to Moosilauke was bitter cold with strong winds. As an alpine zone, there's no tree cover to protect hikers. But at the peak we could finally take shelter in one of several stacked rock cubicles that encircle the summit marker. Warming our numb appendages, we ate our lunch while wearing every layer we had and huddling close together.

Prior to entering New Hampshire, my parents sent back some of our cold gear which we had ditched before leaving the Smoky Mountains (including puffy jackets and rain pants). This would prove critically important from here to the end of the trail.

Within 100 miles, we had left the bugs and swamps of Vermont and entered the frigid highlands, a welcome turn of events indeed!

Throughout the Whites, the alpine terrain sits above the tree line and results in little topsoil and sensitive plant life. This limits hikers to a small swath of trail to prevent further erosion caused by walking in these delicate spaces. It also results in rough and rocky miles. The upside to this is the notable and newfound abundance of grand vistas. This was easily my favorite section of the trail.

That being said, the White Mountains are home to one of the most contentious trail clubs on the entire AT: the Appalachian Mountain Club (AMC).

We had heard a number of rumors before entering the White Mountains, mostly regarding the strictness of camping rules and the absurd expense of the huts. The first half of these rumors turned out to be true, no camping is allowed outside of regulated areas. Likewise, it's true that the AMC huts are quite expensive by thru-hiker standards: around $120 per night for the experience. This included dinner and entertainment, as well as a bunk and vinyl mattress. Luckily, thru-hikers can find their way around this problem with relative ease. The way most often suggested is the "work-for-stay" program. This provides a free dinner and place to stay in exchange for cleaning up after dinner and helping with breakfast in the morning.

The better way of addressing the hut situation, in my opinion, is to use the thru-hiker pass card. Although we knew nothing about this heading into the Whites, it turns out that paying for a site at any of the official AMC campsites grants two more nights at campsites for a reduced price and three free lunchtime snacks at the huts. All of this for the price of $10. In fact, it would turn out that only some of the hut employees would even mark your card after giving out the soup or snacks, which meant that we actually received even more from this card than expected.

Although in practice we avoided staying at the huts as much as possible, it's prudent to stay at just one hut in particular: the Lake of the Clouds. Doing so allows for a timed ascent of Mount Washington in accordance with the weather. Mount Washington, a short hike north from Lake of the Clouds, has the fastest recorded wind speed of anywhere on the planet and can quickly turn into a dangerous situation even in the middle of summer. As thru-hikers, we were given the option to sleep on the floor for $10, a deal we happily agreed to over the alternative. All told, we completed the entire White Mountains section for just $20 each – a drop in the bucket compared to what hearsay would have led us to believe.

• • •

Our first campsite in the Whites was at Liberty Springs, a set of tent pads lined the side of a steep slope about halfway up to Franconia Ridgeline. Like other regulated campsites within the White Mountain range, this site was inhabited by an AMC employee responsible for checking campers into sites and giving them the rundown on rules. These employees lived in large canvas tents for at least a month at a time, rotating through the campsites during the season. This first night staying in the Whites was a different camping experience than we had experienced previously, most notably due to the official oversight and regulated cooking rules that required everyone to use a small, dirty space far from both the tents and the water source to prevent food smells from attracting animals. The campsite also required pitching the tents on raised wooden platforms. These are certainly not my top choice for sleeping – they sleep cold, the wind drawing heat from every angle. I try to avoid these whenever possible; I actually prefer those mouse infested shelters when it comes to getting a good night's sleep.

The next morning would cement itself in our minds as one of the best days on trail, and certainly the one with our favorite mountain landscapes. We had another steep ascent in the morning followed by a cruisy, rolling ridge walk the rest of the day. From the first peak we could see the entire day's hike laid out before us, replete with undulating peaks and saddles which included the summits of Little Haystack, Mt Lincoln, and Mt Lafayette. We couldn't have asked for better weather that day, the skies were clear and blue, the wind surprisingly mild. A glance off the ridgeline in either direction was met by slopes covered in wildflowers sweeping down to the tree covered valleys from which we had climbed the day before.

This was Franconia Ridgeline, the crown jewel of the Whites, and one of the most popular day-hikes in the entire range. Because of this, we would spend the day surrounded by trail runners (who were lucky enough to have this be their training location) and day-hikers who were, more often than not, quite interested in what we were doing. In fact, one notable exchange with a day-hiker went something like this:

Hiker: "That was quite a hike up from the parking lot, but it was well worth it don't you think? Where did you two come from?"

Us: "Georgia, and it was definitely worth it."

Hiker: *loses ability to communicate in full sentences while coming to terms with what we just said*

● ● ●

Much like Mount Moosilauke, the summits here have stacked stone cubicles that provide wind protection for weary hikers. We headed for one of these as we hit the peak of Little Haystack around lunch time. Still talking to some guys out for a trail run as we descended the stairs into one of these cubicles, I took a stumble and smashed my kneecap into the stone. Pain radiated across my body.

My knees are bad enough as it is, having injured them pole vaulting in my younger years. Now I have to worry about a shattered kneecap, great...

I had hit it hard, but I was lucky; this would be one of the few times on the trail that I narrowly dodged a serious injury. That isn't to say it didn't hurt like hell while I slowly ate my lunch and nursed my pride (not to mention my throbbing knee).

As ridge walks in the White Mountains go, Franconia is relatively easy both underfoot and in grade. For the most part, hikers can stroll carefree from summit to summit without shoe gazing as was required in the previous few states. Unobstructed by any dense foliage, the mountains in this area cold be freely viewed from every angle like proud peacocks presenting their plumage. Walking across the rolling peaks, we remembered to look back from time to time and had the pleasure of seeing where we were earlier in the day. Feelings of accomplishment mixed with the pleasure of having perfect weather; that day was especially mild, low winds and temperatures perfect for hiking under slightly overcast skies. Much like my previous experiences of euphoric hiker clarity on Rocky Top, I was awash in a peacefulness which I have come to know as the pinnacle of hiking experience.

Bounding down from the ridge to enter the tree line once more, we came across our first AMC hut. Unlike the lean-tos of the southern trail, these were multi-room cabins powered by solar panel arrays and staffed by a "croo" of 4-6 college age kids. At least, the croo was usually around. In this case, we must have happened upon this first hut during break time because the hut was completely empty save for one hiker sitting in the corner. Lunch had already been served, but the leftovers remained on the counter and a little soup cooled in a pot on the stove. The hiker, already eating, told us to dig in.

I wasn't sure if we should, but I figured we were helping anyway; why, if we didn't finish all these leftovers then someone would be made to carry them back down the mountain, and we couldn't have that!

We carried on this way, resting at huts for lunch and stopping in the evening at the regulated campsites. At Zealand Hut, a day or two later, we used our tickets for free soup and bread. The soup was near boiling, so we thought, "why not add ramen"? That night our bellies were filled with hot food, and were treated to our first experience with the singing and entertainment provided by the huts. I was happy to be sitting away from it all honestly, it appears to be for the kids more than anything.

That night, having come from Zealand Hut after dinner, we found a little patch of flat space and made a stealth camp. Our one and only "illegal" camping site on AMC turf. No one could tell we were there the next morning anyway, and no alpine terrain was hurt in the process.

Soon thereafter, we would approach Mount Washington near the midpoint of the White Mountains. This behemoth of the northern range is known for its wicked weather patterns, blistering wind, and a viewing platform from which you can see endless miles of mountains. For reasons of safety, and the fact that the next legal campsite was many miles from the summit, we decided to quit early the night before and tackle the mountain first thing in the morning. The only reasonable way to achieve a morning summit of Mount Washington was to stay at the Lake of the Clouds, the only hut we would stay in the Whites.

As we approached the hut that evening, we discussed where we would stay and expected that the infamous dungeon would have to do. The man at the desk gave us the option to check out the dungeon first, or we can pay a little more to sleep on the floor of the dining room. I will not mince words here, don't stay in that torture chamber if you have any other choice – the risk of hypothermia is real.

Needless to say, all the thru-hikers chose the dining room floor that evening.

Although our $10 fee didn't buy us dinner, we were treated to (or rather, could not avoid) the entertainment provided by the croo to their higher paying customers. Their experience differed from ours to the tune of one vinyl bunk bed, dinner, and $110. I think thru-hikers got the better deal honestly. For that price we could buy almost two weeks of trail food and I prefer my own inflatable mattress anyway.

The hut was full, and we were treated to stories from overnighters who had made the trip to this hut from all across the country. They played board games and sang songs while the thru-hikers were allocated a single bench in the corner where they could cook their own food and mingle among themselves. To the chagrin of the thru-hikers, the tourists continued to congregate loudly long after hiker midnight had come and gone. We were ready to crash, but we held no power or privilege here.

Thru-hikers should know going into the Whites about the other, more impactful, reason the AMC is sometimes referred to as the Appalachian Money Club. The entire experience in this section panders to these higher paying customers, and your experience will take a back seat to theirs, both in the huts and on the trails. This bias manifests itself most critically as a lack of trail maintenance, namely signage and blazing, in the sections which are frequently used by day-hikers. Even if you wanted to pay more for an experience like theirs, you would likely not be able unless you booked your specific night months in advance – an impossibility for someone whose journey involves more than 100 days of hiking time before reaching these huts. For these reasons, the Whites are a double-edged sword: easily the most beautiful section, but also focused entirely on tourists.

The AMC method of operation is no fluke, it actually has a long history predating the concept of thru-hiking itself. I was surprised to find my own experience in these mountains differed little from the first thru-hike described by Earl Shaffer in 1948. You see, the huts in this region date back to 1876 with the completion of the Lonesome Lake cabin, although it would not be officially added to the AMC system until 1929. The Madison Spring hut was started in 1888 and later became the first AMC hut requiring a fee for a night's stay: the lofty price of 50 cents a head.

The highest, largest, and probably most important hut was built in 1901 in response to the deaths of two hikers on their way to Mount Washington. The Lake of the Clouds, as it would be known, was then, as it is now, a massively popular tourist destination. This hut is itself predated by the famous "Cog" railway, first opened in 1868 for the purpose of carting paying customers to the summit of Washington. By the time Shaffer reached his first AMC hut on the AT, Greenleaf, the practices of the AMC we know (and disdain) today had been in operation for longer than he had been alive. A croo of young adults, about his age, were simply astounded by how far he had walked to reach them. Running low on funds, Shaffer offered to pay the fee at a later date. But the croo firmly rejected; instead, he was offered free passage "in view of his tremendous accomplishment" (so said Pete Walker, Hutmaster).

Keep this in mind while in the AMC territory: we thru-hikers are simply pilgrims passing through. These systems were not designed for us but for the common citizen so that they could enjoy the astounding beauty of this place while avoiding all the effort. By comparison, thru-hikers are a strange breed which has come from the forest to coexist for a short while with the city folk. To some who visit these huts, thru-hikers are as much a part of the lore as the mountains themselves.

● ● ●

The sun came through the large bay windows and met us where we slept on the dining room floor at Lake of the Clouds Hut. Several thru-hikers rose with this warm greeting and prepared to summit Mount Washington before the other hut guests were given their breakfast. It was a brisk and bitter morning, but we had managed to avoid any precipitation. Layered in every piece of clothing we had, including a full rain suit to break the wind, Chilly and I made our way up the winding path past several large, pristine lakes for which the hut is named.

The summit of Washington is a flat plateau which houses a large research facility in addition to a small restaurant, which wouldn't be open for another few hours. The wind cut like a knife, and it was all I could do to catch my breath by walking backwards into the wind.

We didn't stay much longer at the summit than was required to get our pictures and take in a 360° view of the mountain range around us. During more popular times of the day, this area would be flooded with visitors who drove their cars to the summit and would take shelter in the restaurant with a warm beverage. At a close second place behind the elevation at Clingmans Dome, Mount Washington would be our last grand peak before we reached Katahdin. This summit also marked a transition point in the Whites whereafter the trails became far rockier and much more poorly marked. During our descent, we would see the old cog train which runs daily to the top, now carrying supplies. No longer used for its original task of carrying tourists, this old track still climbs without fail – and will likely continue doing so long after I'm gone.

Far fewer day-hikers make it to the side of the range, and our trail would resume its relative solitude because of it. The one exception to this rule came the following day as we reached a saddle between peaks which was covered in wildflowers was met by a well-worn side trail leading off the ridge. Here we would meet a lovely older couple who told us of their long-distance hiking adventures in their younger years. I think they saw something of themselves in us, and we were happy to share that moment with them. The remaining hike that day was a pleasant one, but it would stand in stark contrast to the day that followed.

● ● ●

Our final day in the Whites was a long one. The sky began to dump rain on our head just as we were reaching Monroe, a peak known for its dangerous and rocky descent. This day would mark my grumpiest day on trail; having received mildly bad news from home that morning made our treacherous down climb over slippery rocks in cold rain all the more bitter. I didn't have many days like this on trail, but Chilly was wise enough to fall back a little and let me storm forward in my angry march, cursing everything around me. To be honest, I suppose I needed a little catharsis to get me through. The AMC was just the latest thing to wear on my nerves.

Leaving the White Mountain range, we followed a rushing river wedged between steep rocky slopes covered in dense pine groves. Deep grooves in otherwise slippery rock slabs provided footholds as we worked our way back and forth across the river and down, always and endlessly down. A treacherous descent on a day when the shivers shook my knees and threatened my footing. This was no easy task; but gradually, the trail flattened and the rocks soon gave way to smooth soil. This new section of the trail was freshly maintained, and soon enough we came upon a crew removing rocks from the trail and creating this welcome runway down from the mountains. We thanked them profusely, it had been many days since we walked trails as forgiving as this.

THE HALCYON DAYS OF MAINE

"I took a walk in the woods and came out taller than trees." –Henry David Thoreau

Upon entering Maine's southern section, we were almost immediately met with the single hardest mile on the AT: Mahoosuc Notch. The excitement was palpable, we had waited the whole trail for this day. The night prior was spent near the summit of Fulling Mountain, just south of the notch. We spent that morning descending giant rock slabs still covered in dew. Slipping and sliding between any stable patch of dirt or debris where we could find firm footing.

By the time we reached the notch itself, a small line had formed. You can always cheat and go around, or you can face the best rock climbing and balancing act on the entire trail. We obviously picked the latter.

One by one, hikers crawled like spiders over the first few obstacles. Slower people with larger packs were happy to let us jump in line, especially near the spaces where those large packs needed removing in order to fit through small, claustrophobic "lemon squeezers". We, on the other hand, moved through this section like gymnasts and reveled in the experience. At one point near the middle of this mile, we were met by ice hidden away in a rocky chamber, despite the fact that it was the middle of summer.

After climbing, crawling on hands and knees, doing a plank here or a lunge there, and bum shuffling our way through the notch, we came to a bend in the trail which immediately ran straight back up the next mountain. Taking a breather here, we realized that one mile stretch took about 45 minutes – not bad at all compared to the four hours it takes some!

Next we faced a treacherous climb up the Mahoosuc Arm. This 1500 foot climb is filled with long granite slabs, each having little to no traction. This is considered by some to be even more difficult than the notch proper. I tend to agree. While the notch involved a fun clamber through, over, under, and through obstacles – this climb was simply a balancing act where one false move could send you tumbling 50 feet or more down an unforgiving rock face. At times, we relied on bunched tree debris which lined the "trail", if it could even be called that, as a means to gain traction; a gambit that seemed safer than trusting the smooth stone beneath it.

After much effort, we reached the summit of Old Speck, the original Northern Terminus of the Appalachian Trail, and dropped down to Speck Pond where we could rest our fried nerves. This was one hell of a workout, but we completed it with a sublime satisfaction. Unlike Clingmans Dome in the Smokies, we actually had just completed the most difficult section of the entire trail.

• • •

Our time spent in the woods of Southern Maine was filled with excitement and beauty. We had been reinvigorated after the spectacular White Mountains of New Hampshire and the challenge of Mahoosuc, and now neared the goal of our journey. Or maybe the Northern Terminus is just the end, and the goal was the journey itself. Either way, we would savor these last few weeks.

Southern Maine is filled with lakes and ponds of various sizes dotting the landscape between hills and small mountain peaks. Almost every body of water we crossed dazzled in the sun and provided a beach on which we could take it all in. The natural appeal of this area is great enough that it sparked Henry David Thoreau into writing a book called "The Woods of Maine" about his own experiences traveling through the backwoods and waterways we were now experiencing ourselves.

The secluded wilderness of Maine has all the mystique and romance one could want when sauntering through the mountains, but this comes with a price to thru-hikers. Hitchhiking from the deep backwoods feels only slightly better than being outright lost in the woods; the only difference being the slim possibility a car actually drives these abandoned back roads.

When the time to resupply came, no good option would present itself. The road from which we finally decided to hitch was a small, gravel path practically off the grid. No cars passed in nearly an hour, what a terrible place to wait. We debated moving on, but that would require walking another ten miles or better to the next road and we had all but depleted our rations. Just when we were about to give up, a little red car crept slowly around the corner.

What were the chances we would get a hitch on the first car? Not great.

And yet, amazingly, he stopped and gave us a lift. Even more incredible, I actually knew this man. Not that we had met, but I was quite familiar with the research of our kindly driver; Dr. Thomas Seeley, an expert in honey bees, on his way home from giving a lecture. If you're not familiar with the rich history of honeybee science, you may not recognize his name and, if this is the case, I assure you that you're missing out on something special. As far as I was concerned, I had found a living legend out here in the middle of nowhere. I couldn't believe my luck, I had studied his work in both undergrad and graduate school, and I didn't let the opportunity to pick his brain pass me by.

After Dr. Seeley dropped us off in Andover, we made our resupply stop, and were off again. Another quick hitch took us back to the trail, and a short jaunt later we were climbing Sugarloaf Mountain. Although this is a popular ski destination, we care more about this mountain due to its position at, roughly, the 2000 mile mark for NOBO thru-hikers. No fewer than five hiker-made mile markers lined the trail here; made of stones, sticks, and bark, the excitement of our fellow hikers matched our own upon achieving this distance. The end was nigh, a reminder to savor every last moment.

While gallivanting through this unpopulated wilderness, we came across a small, off the grid hostel just off trail a few hundred yards: The Hiker Hut. While the name is reminiscent of the giant tourist traps of New Hampshire, this hidden gem could not have been more different. With only a few portable solar panels and a stream for running water, this was just a small hippy campsite encircled by a handful of small, handmade cabins. Each cabin had a unique design and paint job, one with a giant daisy beautifying its tin roof, and not any bigger than a mid-sized camper.

The shower was at once magical and a small scale ecological disaster. Standing naked between a few large bushes and the rushing river, my shower water heated by propane after being bucket drawn straight from the river itself. I love showers for the ability to stimulate introspection and calming mindfulness; and coupled with a mountainous backdrop bubbling river, I was in ecstasy.

Chilly and I would spend the evening just a little further down the river, in a three-sided hut open to the water. The little room was a romantic setting, complete with flowing white curtains as our door, the gurgling stream to soothe us into sleep, and a mosquito net surrounding the bed to keep us bug free. Ah yes, the romance of a bug net; how my standards had changed!

I was laying on the soft bed in the afterglow of my shower when Chilly returned from her own. She couldn't believe they were letting the soap just wash straight into the river, and I completely agreed.

Sometimes you just have to make the best of the things you can't change.

•••

A few days after leaving the Hiker Hut we came to the Kennebec River, notorious for being the only river that can't be crossed without assistance. Knowing what we were looking for, but not sure what to expect, we eventually stumbled our way out of the woods and onto a small beach. Across the river sat a man in a lawn chair, eating his lunch; he waved and shouted that we should write our names in the log book and he would be over in a minute. That minute lasted long enough for us to sit down and eat our own snacks until the canoe finally pushed off and made its way to our side of the river. Long and green, with enough space for three, the man at the helm beckoned us to join him in his "pickle boat", and don some life jackets. He and I paddled our way back across while Chilly relaxed and film the crossing. Once to the other side, we hopped out and bid him farewell as he returned to his lawn chair and opened another beer.

A few hundred feet down trail we reached what would be our last bed and shower on the entire trail: Caratunk House. A cozy, multi-story house with private bedrooms and a family dining table where the guests could congregate. In addition, there was a storeroom where thru-hikers could restock, or find microwave pizzas for dinner; and above that a bunk room for overflow. We enjoyed both the company in the evening and our private room for the night.

Before entering the 100 Mile Wilderness, we needed to make the last restock of the AT. Most choose to go east to Monson, which is closer than the westward option of Greenville, but which has a much more limited grocery selection. So we chose Greenville, a choice which would set into motion our most dodgy hitch to date. We should have seen it coming before we even got in the car.

An elderly gentleman drove the small sedan, his middle-aged son in the passenger seat. Upon seeing us with our thumbs in the air, they swerved dramatically toward the curb without fully exiting their lane on this small mountain road. This wouldn't have been much of a problem if a semi-truck would not have been so close on their tail. It swerved across the midline to avoid smashing our would-be lift. Somehow we reasoned, "This will be fine right?" and hopped in the back seat.

We spent the next 20 minutes listening to the adventures of this father and son pair while careening obliviously through traffic. Once we got into town, our generous driver pulled into the grocery store parking lot, abruptly cutting off an oncoming RV whose driver threw his hands up in disgust. From the passenger seat, the son waved his apology while his father, chipper as could be, never even noticed.

Even though we had hitchhiked 30 times or better, we never had a dangerous encounter such as this. If I ever need to hitchhike again, I will try to be more discriminating!

Once back on trail, we had only a few days left and excitedly picked up our pace. Eventually, we would climb on to our last major mountain before the end and see from its rocky, bald top the not so distant goal of our summer, and of my childhood. Laid out before us was a long, low valley – the only thing standing between this perch and our final destination: Mount Katahdin. We recognized it immediately, with its broad shoulders standing alone, dwarfing the surrounding landscape. Thinking of that moment now makes my spine tingle.

We stood awestruck before a legend. It felt like coming home.

● ● ●

The 100 Mile Wilderness stands as the last major challenge before reaching the base of Katahdin. Technically speaking, this is the most remote section of the Appalachian Trail. A sign at its trailhead warns hikers to have at least ten days of food.

We packed just four.

By this point, my trail confidence was at an all-time high. This was also our longest time between grocery stores that we would experience, and I didn't want to pack a ton of weight in food. My solution, resulting from these two facts, would be to survive mostly on Snickers bars. This would save weight and, as my confidence assured me, would be totally fine for my nutritional needs.

It became clear by day three that I still had something to learn about hiker nutrition, as my diet of Snickers bars could not stave off the insatiable hiker hunger. This resulted in "hangry" arguments with the mosquitoes who pestered me for the first time since Vermont. They weren't even slightly phased by my cursing their very existence.

Other than the bugs, and the lack of impressive peaks found in the mountain ranges from which we had just come, the 100 Mile Wilderness is still uniquely beautiful. Numerous large lakes speckle this forest and can be viewed from small rock outcroppings that periodically poke out from the canopy. This area is commonly used for boating and tours by pontoon planes which come and go from the lakes throughout the day.

Beaver dams were also quite common here, and added to the large population of ponds in Maine. At one particularly large beaver dam, the trail was diverted around the outside and up an extra hill we could have otherwise avoided. This beaver pond must have been about the size of a football field, and in it we could see a handful of beavers going about their business. Interestingly, the pond was patrolled by one enormous beaver the entire time we were near, while three smaller beavers worked on felling a tree across the pond from our position. Such industry and creative construction from some of my favorite woodland critters; such a pleasure to see.

Although we had seen several SOBO thru-hikers prior to the 100 Mile Wilderness, it became clear in this section of the trail that the SOBO season approached its own bubble. Comparing NOBO to SOBO thru-hikers at this stage is a little like comparing me to a bodybuilder, making all the more obvious the degree to which a complete thru-hike grants, or forces, a high degree of athleticism. Chilly and I bounded like deer up the rock faces only to meet SOBOs huffing and puffing, yet to develop their own trail legs.

It also became clear that many SOBOs had yet to learn any trail etiquette. One night while sleeping peacefully, I awoke to one of them walking past me with her white headlamp fully ablaze and pointed directly at my face. You have a red light filter for exactly this reason – USE IT!

The flat terrain in this section allowed us to cover many miles each day. Combine that with our peak physical fitness here in the final state on the AT, we averaged marathon distances on consecutive days all the way through the 100 mile wilderness.

● ● ●

The night before entering Baxter State Park, home of Mount Katahdin, we stayed at Rainbow Stream lean-to roughly 25 miles from the base of the final mountain. We woke early that morning and rushed through the first 15 miles to the park border where we knew a sign-up sheet would await. Thru-hikers expecting to stay within Baxter State Park are required to camp at the Birches campsite, limited to 12 people per day. In order to reserve a spot, thru-hikers need to add their name to this list located ten miles out. However, upon reaching the sign in sheet we would find we were too late. In fact, we were beaten to the punch by 12 other hikers who apparently slept at the nearby motel in order to sign this sheet at 7AM. Dismayed at what this might mean for our summit hopes the next day, we nonetheless skipped exuberantly toward our goal.

Arriving at the Baxter campground that afternoon, we were greeted by my parents who had driven to Maine in order to celebrate our impending accomplishment. They informed us that we had just missed the Corey family who had summited the day before us and left Baxter earlier this morning. Disappointed after having missed them, I was still overjoyed they had made it. They had started the trail a day before us and ended a day before us as well; always a pleasure, I will never forget them.

Apparently, it was their youngest son, Yahoo, who had found my parents just by way of his outgoing personality. My dad was apparently tightening a screw on his glasses when Yahoo ran right up to him and took a close look.

"Hey, did you break your glasses? Did ya fall down!?"

My dad told him he was just making them fit better while he waited on his son to get here.

Yahoo must have known immediately that this man's son was a thru-hiker, "Hey I'm a thru-hiker too! That's my family over there".

My dad recognized the family immediately from my stories: three kids, the parents, and the grandparents in a camper van following them up the trail. So while we did not get to say goodbye directly, at least my parents met them and could congratulate them on their accomplishment.

Beside this touching story, my parents had also brought a gourmet picnic which lifted our mood. Good thing too, we were about to walk into a conversation fully expecting to be denied a decent campsite for our last night on trail. If this occurred, it would likely mean we were headed an hour and a half south of the mountain to stay in a hotel room with my parents. Not the sendoff of our dreams.

As we approached the ranger station, we interrupted a rather aggressive conversation aimed at our friends Kentucky and Jeff. The ranger was clearly having a bad day, and this negatively impacted our friends who were just hoping to find a place to stay the night. Perhaps risking our own chances, Chilly and I popped ourselves down at the picnic bench and attempted to lighten the mood with a cheery reunion between friends separated hundreds of miles ago.

Somehow, our buddies ended up with a place to stay that night. Then the attention shifted to us. As it turned out, only 11 people had checked in so far that day and thus one spot was open at the Birches. Of course, Chilly and I refused to separate for our last night and we told the ranger as much. He spent the next ten minutes rummaging through papers trying to find a way for us to stay. We sat there with smiles and hope on our faces as the ranger continually looked between us and his documents. He must have counted the number of campers five or six times, coming to the same conclusion every time but the last.

He had found us a way to stay.

Maybe it was as he said, simply a calculation error on his part. However, I choose to believe it was just a little bit of extra trail magic shared between a ranger who held absolute power and a happy couple just hoping to finish their journey the way they had imagined it.

An air of relief fell over our group sitting there at the picnic table and the ranger, now as cheery as we were, assigned us our final northbound numbers: thru-hikers 411 and 412 to summit Katahdin that year.

We bid my parents good evening, and they wished us good luck in the morning assuring us they would return before we came down from the mountain. The campsite was a bit of a walk off trail, and by the time we arrived no less than 15 other campers were already there. It turned out the restrictions were not as strictly enforced as we were led to believe. But don't tell them I told you that.

• • •

"You're off to great places, today is your day. Your mountain is waiting, so get on your way."
-Dr. Seuss

The next morning was a bright and crisp day. We broke camp early and made our way back to the main campground. The trail leading to the summit involves five miles up, and a return trip back down; though some people do choose to take one of the alternate routes off the mountain, such as the precarious Knife's Edge.

The first one or two miles of this approach is deceptively easy and includes a glittering waterfall at its conclusion. This makes it a destination for day-hikers of any skill level. To press beyond the waterfall requires increasing skill and athleticism for each additional mile. First are the rock steps which remind me of the climb up to Mount Lafayette. Scrambling up and around boulders was only a preview of what would come next. Only once we had climbed above the tree line did we comprehend the magnitude of our final ascent. Before us lay an astounding vertical climb, one of the most difficult on the entire trail.

Soon we were facing featureless rock faces ten to 15 feet tall, the only accessible route included embedded rebar hooks for a foot or hand. At one point, we approached a group of day-hikers attempting to scale these cliffs. We came upon them just as three of the men were pushing and dragging their female companion up the wall while she appeared to be having a panic attack. Although unfortunate, it's not a surprising occurrence; these heights could induce vertigo in anyone the least bit susceptible. Ten minutes of must have passed before the woman reached a safe space where she could catch her breath. Her companions urged us to pass. They were in the middle of offering us a hand up when Chilly grasped a rebar hold and cleared the obstacle in a single bound. Astonished, the day-hikers confirmed to each other that we must have been in much better shape than them while I performed a similar maneuver.

We continued this way for at least a mile and a half, having a rock climbing adventure reminiscent of Mahoosuc Notch, but completely vertical and with the endless alpine views of the White Mountains.

It was glorious. A challenge suited for our trail hardened minds and bodies, fit for our half year pilgrimage north.

Then suddenly the hard part was over. We stepped up one last time onto an expansive plateau from which we could just make out the sign at the Northern Terminus. But this plateau was a challenge of a different kind. The wind was so strong it pulled the breath from my lungs and threatened to rip my hat from its perch on my pack. I began to get a bit anxious, shaky even, and we picked up our pace at the sight of that famous brown sign we had walked towards for almost five months.

As we approached the sign, cheers were mounted by hikers already at the summit. Most of them were day-hikers, but we recognized a few familiar faces among the others. Together, Chilly and I made our way up the rock mound surrounding the summit and ceremoniously touched the finish line. Ice cold wood, surrounded by a sea of fog, resting quietly on jagged rocks.

We had done it, and we had done it together.

The truth of it settled in over the next few minutes as we were surrounded by John and several other thru-hikers, sharing our congratulations and the astonishment at the achievement we had all just completed. Sitting there at the summit, basking in the glory of it all, eating the last trail snacks we would need for a while.

A relaxing calm settled over me: other than getting down

from the mountain, there was nowhere left to go, no more restocking food or recharging batteries, no more worrying about bad weather or the ticks and mosquitoes; but no more moments like this either I suppose.

This last realization would stick with me, indefinitely as far as I can tell.

Chilly had similar feelings, a mix of exuberance and sadness at being finished. We joked that walking all the way back to Georgia was an option. I think she was just waiting for me to dare her.

Soon enough, Jeff and Kentucky made their way up the final ascent. We began to cheer and clap as those before us had done, and they raised their hands in triumph before placing them on the sign. We each stood on the sign and took our completion photos, as was tradition. We gathered for a group photo, and we shared this moment with our friends – perhaps the last time we would see each other. But no one said it.

I think we were all struck with the thought, "What now?"

Despite the fact that I had numerous plans laid out after 143 days of thinking and planning, the feeling of being lost without another blaze to follow was nearly overwhelming.

I think back now to that moment and know that I realized a truth that day. For as long as I could remember I had thought of this moment, but upon getting here, it became glaringly obvious that Katahdin was little more than the end to an adventure of a lifetime. Another grand mountain, another brown sign etched in my memory.

But it's the adventure itself, both its successes and hardships, and the people with whom I shared this experience that I will remember forever.

EPILOGUE: POST TRAIL, MARRIAGE, AND OUR NEXT ADVENTURE

"We never can part with it; the mind loves its old home: as water to our thirst, so is the rock, the ground, to our eyes, and hands, and feet." – Ralph Waldo Emerson

During the two months following our completion of the trail, our physical activity and level of daily novelty went from 100 to 0 practically overnight. In 2019, a total of 4046 thru-hiking attempts were reported on the Appalachian Trail. Of these, only 20.6% (833) reported completion of the entire trail. We had completed a challenge that few others have even attempted, and fewer still have completed. We were among good company.

And yet, we were faced with two immediate problems that cut short our celebratory vibe: first, Chilly needed to leave for Canada to begin her work visa. This included finding a job with an engineering firm. Second, I needed to find a way to join her and get my own income up and running. I began with science writing to generate some income, this was something that I could continue after crossing the border.

Having been to Canada a handful of times throughout my life, I expected no problem following her across the border. I even confirmed this with all the online documentation I could find. My experience this time, however, more closely mirrored that of a suspected criminal. I was accused of attempting to overstay my visa before ever entering the country.

Eventually, after enough kind argument, they granted me just six weeks and told me to leave just before Christmas. Needless to say, my opinion of our neighbors to the north soured somewhat that day.

Regardless, those six weeks were wonderful. We spent them playing house and, more to the point, testing the strength of our relationship off the trail. This was a prerequisite for the both of us, and the only thing that stopped me from proposing on Mount Katahdin.

It's really quite funny looking back at our apprehension from this future standpoint. From an outside perspective, it may appear that everything moved unrealistically fast. Some of that same sentiment certainly led to our hesitation.

We shouldn't have allowed it to do so.

Even now I'm often asked when I first knew that she was the one. Honestly, I think I may have felt that way before she did, but not by much. The answer now is obvious to us both – almost immediately.

• • •

After leaving Canada against my will, I headed to upstate New York where I had planned to start my small business in the early spring. Until then I would prepare.

Chilly had found a job by this point, and luckily, was able to get time off over the holidays. I didn't want to risk attempting to go back to Canada so soon, so she would come down to visit me in New York. By the time this plan was in place, I had already bought the ring and only needed to find the right time and place to ask. I chose a location which fit our relationship well: Letchworth State Park near the New York Finger Lakes. We found ourselves, on Boxing Day in the year we first met, on a snow covered bridge there in New York – me on one knee.

It caught her completely off guard, but there was no hesitation in her voice. In fact, I could barely finish my sentence before she said "yes".

We had just a week left to celebrate our engagement before she needed to head back across the border. I knew then that I would need to follow her as soon as I could.

• • •

I spent the next two months apart from her establishing some cash flow. I continued my science writing, added online tutoring, and returned to an old hobby of mine from grad school – options trading. Boy was I in for a wild ride in 2020. On one hand, I would leave the States in February just two weeks before the global Coronavirus pandemic led to the borders being closed. On the other hand, I had decided to reinvolve myself in the stock market at the very end of the best bull market in history. My timing was both impeccable and terrible.

I returned to Chilly on Valentine's Day, using the visa waiver program to get six months this time around. We had just two weeks before the pandemic hit to get in some skiing and rock climbing. I think this helped sustain us after the shelter-in-place orders came into effect. Soon, like many others who were lucky enough to be in such a position, both Chilly and I were working from home, together.

Other than the pandemic, our biggest challenge now was finding a way to live together long-term. Even though we were engaged and could get married at any point, we were faced with the harsh reality of the United States green card system. Completely unlike the movies or political ads, getting married is no golden ticket for entry to the United States. This process takes no less than a year and a half, and it comes with numerous strings attached. We started the process at the beginning of 2020 and still are in the first of several phases at the end of the year. We're now weighing our options for the next step; but one thing is for certain, we won't get split up again.

Our next adventure takes us to New Zealand where we will be able to marry. We realized all too late that a courthouse wedding would have allowed us to stay together in Canada. But like I said earlier, we were trying not to rush things when we should have just realized right away that it was the real deal and dove in head first.

Visiting New Zealand has been a goal of mine for many years, I never imagined I would be doing it as my honeymoon after getting married to a Kiwi.

Of course, an American visiting New Zealand during a global pandemic is no easy task. Not to mention the fact that the U.S. response has been among the worst in the world while New Zealand celebrates having zero community cases in their country (as I write). Luckily, I was granted a border closure exemption to visit the country based on my relationship with Chilly.

As we prepare to embark on this journey together, we sit on opposite sides of a closed border waiting to reunite and leave the country just before one of the most contentious American elections in history. Our readiness to get away from North America for a bit, get married, and just enjoy our lives together could not be overstated.

I write this now while walking around the woods of Ohio, separated from my partner and thinking of little more than hiking with her again. It's the best I can do to recreate the trail experience in my mind and provide you with this story.

Our plan now is a rather simple one, but it returns us to our roots as a couple. Over the course of four to six months we will travel New Zealand in a camper van, visiting some of the world's best trails and living minimally and with purpose. The lessons in minimalism and frugality have clearly translated to post-trail life for us, and we continue to take joy in simple living even during the complex times our world now faces.

If you seek to hike a long trail as well, I only want for you to experience an adventure of the magnitude that we did, and I would love for you to reach out to me and let me know how I can help; or maybe just tell me about your own experience. If you have already completed a long trail yourself, I hope that our story has provided you with the same soothing nostalgia that I gained by writing it.

This was also written for our children, not yet born, who will eventually read this story about how their parents met and will wonder about the great adventures we had. Likewise for myself and Chilly, this story shall stand the test of time while our interpretation shifts with the coming years. But perhaps the insights gained with more time to reflect will be no less consequential.

And if you're reading this but have no interest, or no ability, to hike long trails yourself, I hope you were at least able to imagine yourself hiking alongside us on our way to Katahdin.

Thanks For Reading!

If you have enjoyed reading our story, it would benefit us greatly if you could provide an honest review on this book's store page.

If you want more of this story, the entire adventure was captured on video and published to YouTube. Search: <u>Chilly Bin Hikes</u>

For more information aimed at the hiking community directly, read on. Appendix A addresses the often overlooked issues of post-trail mental health that many members of our community face, while Appendix B will provide detailed information that future thru-hikers will likely find useful.

APPENDIX A – POST TRAIL MENTAL HEALTH IN THE THRU-HIKING COMMUNITY

Thru-hiking is, without a doubt, one of the pinnacles of personal achievement for anyone who succeeds; it often leads to some of the best and most memorable experiences in a person's life. However, reaching such heights of human experience must also, inevitably, involve walking back down that mountain – a feat that many find far more challenging than the accomplishment itself.

Although post-trail mental health is being discussed more frequently now than it was in the past, much more work is needed to address this topic; therefore, I will present here a brief overview of the issues, several potential solutions, and discuss where we, as a trail community, might go from here.

First, let me define the problem. It's sometimes called post-trail depression; but other, more specific terms may also apply. There is a rather poignant short story passed among thru-hikers authored by Kristin Marie; it's a perfect metaphor for returning from a thru-hike and I will share it here in its entirety:

"Being a thru-hiker is like being a captive orca, born and raised in a tank at Sea World. One day you are put in one of those ocean pens, the big ones for orcas they want to try to rehabilitate and return to the wild. For the first time in your life, you're in the ocean! You're home and, while not completely free, you can sense how big and wild it is. You have room to move, room you never realized you lacked back in the tank. You live out there for five months, interacting with other orcas (also from Sea World) and other marine creatures. You can't live fully free in the ocean because you would die out there; you

have no idea how to survive totally on your own, but you can sense how vast it is, how amazing life would be if you were free. You feel so alive, no longer having to perform tricks for trainers and crammed in such a small, lifeless space.

Then, one day, you're put back in the tank. And you suddenly realize that your entire life you've been captive, trained to perform tricks in a small, crowded tank devoid of life except for other captive orcas. The other orcas ask you how your trip was, what it was like. You have no idea how to describe what you experienced and no idea how to tell them what you know now. To tell them there is so much more to life outside the tank, that they are unwitting prisoners unable to live full lives like wild orcas. You're depressed, but they tell you to get used to being back in the tank, that this is the REAL world and that pen in the ocean was just something fun you did that one time.

But you know. You felt the tides, met incredible creatures, and were no longer controlled by trainers. And every once in a while another orca comes back and you look at each other and wonder... How do we get out this tank? And how do we wake up the others?"

Causes of Post-Trail Depression.

Although it doesn't impact every thru-hiker, it does appear to influence most in some way. How could it not? A thru-hiker returns home to a comparatively sedentary lifestyle, is exposed to less novelty and nature in their daily life, and spends that time around people who generally have little understanding of what the thru-hiker has just experienced. Moreover, some thru-hikers go from being purposefully homeless on the trail, yet perfectly at home, to being actually homeless after having sold everything they own. All of these things are a recipe for a bad mental state.

Perhaps the worst part of all this is that prospective thru-hikers appear to expect only the best during and after their thru-hike, then are subsequently blindsided by the reality. I performed an initial poll in two separate thru-hiking groups, the 2019 class one year after finishing and the 2021 class who were still in preparation for the next season, using around 50 people each. I described the results in Appendix B under Preparation; but suffice it to say that the results were striking, it appears the vast majority of thru-hikers are heading onto the trail expecting no negative consequences to their life circumstances and mental health. Completely in opposition to this, the poll of successful thru-hikers suggests that more than half are impacted, in some sense, by what we call post-trail depression.

• • •

"If a person doesn't want to re-engage at all in their life, they don't want to do things that they previously enjoyed, they are isolating themselves from people, they don't want to get a job, they are having suicidal thoughts, they're coping with substance abuse, or if they're feeling down, depressed or blue." Listed as signs of depression after a thru-hike, written by Dr. Chidester

The only issue with the above is the overlap these signs have with long-sought after forms of spiritual attainment (with the obvious exception of drugs and suicidal thoughts, which are real problems) including, most notably, the Buddhist tradition. I'm not going to spend time here explaining Buddhism's long history with withdrawal from society and seeking happiness from within rather than from without. Instead, let me put it in terms the modern American thru-hiker likely understands all too well. Thru-hiking tends to strip one's values down to their very core, we quickly learn what really matters in life and how little we need to be happy when we're awash in simplicity and deprivation. Thru-hikers then spend the next several months living that truth, and for most, it's among the best times of their life.

Then they return and most are faced with the prospect of needing more money and more stuff to live a generally less fulfilling life than they had on the trail. They are required, in most cases, to work 40+ hours per week at jobs they probably don't love. Granted, some find careers that give them everything they ever wanted. But that is just not the case for most in our society, and the rest are left just trying to get to the weekend so they can enjoy what little time they have left. This is not the path to happiness, and it's made all the more obvious to those who have been through a massive mental and physical undertaking such as a thru-hike. Compounding this issue, thru-hikers may find the people they return to are often less than receptive. After all, you have just gotten back from the adventure of a lifetime, while the people back home have done little more than worked that job.

"After hiking 20 miles per day, a cubicle can feel like a prison. After focusing on nothing but walking, the multitasking of various projects can feel overwhelming. After spending all day outside, the process of going from your home to your car to the office feels unnatural." -Jennifer Pharr Davis

Beyond the social difficulties of returning from the trail, there is also a person detachment from who you were on trail. This phenomenon has been described by Dr. Anne Baker as post-trail grief. She defines thru-hiking as having a particular SPACE (Simplicity/Structure, Purpose, Adventure/Adversity, Community, Extreme Exercise/Endorphins) and suggests that this post-trail grief is caused by: "*1) reluctance to let go of the trail SPACE that facilitated a valued way of being oneself, and 2) reluctance to stop being that version of oneself. Hikers deeply value who they are when they live in the present moment with purpose, community, effort, and openness to uncertainty.*"

The grief caused by losing the trail, in addition to a part of the person who hiked it, is exacerbated by the inability to live life to its fullest in the way that was discovered while hiking.

But another aspect to leaving the trail which also impacts all thru-hikers in one way or another, and it's mentioned above in the discussion of "SPACE"; namely, the abrupt transition from the greatest physical shape you have experienced to a relatively sedentary lifestyle devoid of daily endorphin release. Endorphins, released from one's own body during sustained physical activity, activate the same receptors as opioids and are responsible for the "runner's high" that is shared among all extreme athletes, thru-hikers included. This daily influx of natural mood lifting biochemicals is a major reason climbing mountains is so fun; however, most of us will sustain this "habit" for several months before stopping cold turkey. Even if you try to replace long-distance hiking with other forms of physical activity, every thru-hiker knows that nothing compares.

Caloric intake and expenditure is a secondary, but no less impactful, biological change that takes place after leaving the trail. After spending months taking in two or three times the normal daily caloric requirement, we abruptly stop using those calories while our body is still giving off signals to eat more and more. In many thru-hikers, this results in post-trail weight gain. I was lucky to avoid the weight gain, my metabolism has always been something of an anomaly; nonetheless, I did experience the withdrawal of endorphins like everyone else.

"I did not expect it to last quite so long or be this rough...Right now I'm questioning whether I'm actually better off for having done it, but I know that once I'm through this part in the end it will have been one of the most incredible experiences of my life." -Stormchaser

Such experiences are not completely without precedent; in fact, very similar causes and outcomes can be observed in two other groups as well, 1. retired professional or college athletes and, 2. retired military veterans. Both of these groups experience long periods of vigorous physical activity, simplicity, and varying degrees of veneration among the population. Upon retiring, they, like thru-hikers, may face grief at the loss of who they were on either the playing field or the battle field, a loss of simplicity and direction, and trouble integrating into society at large when their experiences are so unique, vivid, and potentially life altering. This is not to say that all athletes and veterans face depression, clearly nor do all thru-hikers; but it is to say that chances of depression are increased in these populations. There are far more studies in these populations from which our community may draw insight; if you would like to dig deeper you might start with "The effect of depression on the association between military service and life satisfaction" by Britton, Ouimette, and Bossarte 2016, or "Susceptibility for Depression in Current and Retired Student Athletes" by Weigand, Cohen, and Merenstein 2013.

In summation, it appears that post-trail depression is a combination of social estrangement, personal grief in response to a loss of self and state of being, and biochemical withdrawal. Once we start to nail down some of the causes, we can then start to find solutions.

Solutions.

How can a thru-hiker avoid, or diminish, the symptoms of post-trail depression while also integrating the insights gained from life on trail? There are a few suggestions from the literature, or from other thru-hikers; and I will share my own as well.

First, I strongly suggest you start thinking about it early (if you are a prospective thru-hiker). I'm not saying don't go if you don't have a plan, the trail provides plenty of time to think; but you should address the possibility that immediately returning to work will diminish your happiness and lead you towards post-trail depression. Know that the trail will cause changes in perspective, if nothing else; but the changes will come. Optimally, you would form a plan that allows time after the trail to mentally digest what you just accomplished, to form some clear take away messages for yourself to live by, then find a way to integrate what you have learned on the trail back into your post-trail life. Establish healthy habits using those perspectives formed on the trail, before broader society influences and forces your back into the rat race way of thinking. Integrating the experience, rather than disassociating from your trail self, provides more meaning to the thru-hike itself but also more satisfaction in daily life off the trail.

Stay connected to the thru-hiking community; both the specific people with whom you hiked, and the trail community at large. Staying connected was easy when I had shared the experience with my partner, and we were almost immediately thrust into the next set of challenges. These aspects of post-trail life, staying connected to the community and setting new challenges, were discussed extensively in "Appalachian Trials" by Zach Davis – a book well worth reading (as I did prior to my own thru-hike).

This idea of having the next goal ready to go is certainly a good one; however, I had plenty of post-trail plans and still found myself lacking the motivation to start most of them for almost a year. I had everything going for me when I left the trail, subsequently got engaged, and yet I was still affected by a loss of creative motivation until I started writing this book. Some of this was clearly due to a global pandemic and extreme political upheaval, but not all of it. The notes for this manuscript, which I was so excited to write when I was on the trail, sat on my desktop for a full year before I started in earnest. One thing I know for sure, the trail gave me mental freedom and adaptability to a greater extent than I ever had before. Even so, it was difficult to sustain that after the hike was over.

The loss of a sense of self, or detachment from our trail name and persona, is also a widely reported effect of finishing a thru-hike and returning to "normal" life. Dr. Anne Baker's work focuses primarily on this grief aspect, and on the loss of identity; or in other words, the loss of who you were on the trail. To address this loss she suggests bringing who you were on the trail back home with you; finding who you were in the trail SPACE, and determining how that version of you fits into normal life back home.

"The key isn't to find a way to go back to the trail, to recreate what you had. The key is to take what you had, and bring it in your everyday life. Do so, and you'll find that life beyond the trail can be just as exciting and fulfilling as life back on it." -Seeker

This idea of grief being a major component of post-trail depression is incredibly insightful; but the other causes are no less impactful, even if they are below the level of cognition. The aspect which I would find most interesting to probe further is that of addiction. Chilly and I both were perhaps more impacted by the sudden withdrawal from endorphins, due to significantly reduced physical activity, as well as being removed from natural environments more generally - thrust instead into apartment buildings in areas devoid of mountains. Our post-trail slump more closely modelled that of withdrawal than of grief.

To this point, you should have a plan in place to wean yourself off of daily endorphins, rather than going cold turkey. Keep in mind that running daily is very different from hiking daily; don't give yourself an injury chasing the runner's high. That being said, do something that will boost endorphins at least a little bit, and do it frequently.

A major message I want you to see in this section is that it can happen to anyone, it does happen to many, and thru-hiker hopefuls should know that it's a possibility for them too. The exact effects will vary from hiker to hiker, but almost all are likely to feel the endorphin withdrawal at the very least. Having a plan in place before finishing the trail, and putting it into action immediately after the trail, should be a higher priority than attempting to fit back into American work culture and other societal norms. Make sure to focus on yourself first, integrate the trail self with the non-trail self, and do your best to continue living the best possible life complete with all the insights gained from your grand adventure.

If all else fails, take heart in the fact that almost everything is a matter of perspective. Flip your perspective on its head and find new purpose as Mr. Fuller did in this short tale:

"Instead of ending his life, Fuller decided to live from then on as if he had died that night. Being dead, he wouldn't have to worry about how things worked out any longer for himself personally and would be free to devote himself to living as a representative of the universe. The rest of his life would be a gift. Instead of living for himself, he would devote himself to asking, 'what is it on this planet that needs doing that I know something about, that probably won't happen unless I take responsibility for it?' He decided he would just ask that question continuously and do what came to him, following his nose. In this way, working for humanity as an employee of the universe at large, you get to modify and contribute to your locale by who you are, how you are, and what you do. But it's no longer personal. It's just part of the totality of the universe expressing itself." -Jon Kabat-Zinn

What's next?

Each year more and more people attempt to thru-hike long trails around the world. Almost all of them are likely to approach these great endeavors with bright eyes and bushy tails. It's really quite beautiful. This hope, and the unique, life altering nature of this adventure creates one of the most vibrant and free spirited communities on the planet. I'm honored to be considered a member.

But as I've explained above, I believe this is a vulnerable population with an unmet mental health need of unknown magnitude. The neuroscientist in me demands to know more, gather more data, and give something back to this community. We need both pre-trail and post-trail data from people hiking the trail, more transparency, and more abundant information available to new thru-hikers.

For this reason, I will soon be starting a project to study this phenomenon; I want to know how widespread it is, how it manifests, and what we can do to prevent it altogether. The experience of thru-hiking should be nothing but positive; with any luck, we can make that true for everyone.

• • •

If you have interest in participating with such a study, know someone who may be thru-hiking soon or has thru-hiked in the past, or are a scientist in a related field who would like to be involved: please reach out to me, and keep an eye out for this next project that will require large community involvement for success.

You can contact me by email at:
RaidenATnineteen@gmail.com

APPENDIX B – PRACTICAL LESSONS ON LONG DISTANCE SAUNTERING

Preparation

A common question posed in hiker groups is about training prior to a thru-hike. This question comes in two main forms: 1. does physical preparation matter once I hit the trail, and 2. how much backpacking experience should I have before attempting a thru-hike? I will address both of these questions here, but my short summation is that yes preparation matters, but people still sometimes manage to go from inexperienced couch potato to successful thru-hiker. Just don't expect that approach to have a high probability of success.

The only reason to not do some level of physical preparation before thru-hiking is if you believe the common wisdom that everyone is in great shape a month into it anyway, which is mostly true. But, you have to make it through that month of non-stop hiking first. It's in the first month when many hikers leave the trail, such that around half quit before Damascus Virginia. Many factors contribute to this high failure rate at the beginning of the trail, but a large percentage of them are injuries or other physical difficulties.

> *"Even if you devote your life 100% to physically preparing, it still won't get you into the shape the trail will, but getting a head start is going to pay off tremendously."* –Gusha, Hiker Feed

Being physically fit prior to a major physical activity would be taken for granted in nearly every other domain: running, mountaineering, triathlons, you name it. There is more reason for training than wanting to do better than the competition, being physically fit reduces the chance of injury. It does so by increasing endurance, which helps prevent fatigue based injuries, as well as making our movements more efficient and accurate.

Chilly and I both began the trail in good shape and were able to begin hiking mileage in the mid to high teens while the average hiker completes just 8-10 miles per day at the beginning. This led to a fairly flat daily mileage chart from start to finish for us (with a minor bump up after the Smokies). Is this desirable or simply a meaningless side effect? It may be little more than preference, but it could contribute to lower costs on food and town stays if your mileage is higher. Determine for yourself if anything I have mentioned here is worth it. I think the safety alone is enough reason for training, not to mention that anything which reduces strain while walking up mountains on a hot day is a good thing!

Anyone who has done much hiking will confirm that the best training for long-distance hiking is, in fact, long-distance hiking. Sometimes this is said with an air of resignation and leads people to essentially winging it on trail. I would argue that you should do the next best thing. Hike as much as you can and supplement that with gym training targeting muscle groups that are the most used while backpacking. The stair stepper was my gym-machine of choice, but I also focused on my core, knee-stabilizing muscles, ankle stabilizers, and the trapezius to give more padding where my pack would rest. Chilly prepared entirely on trails, getting out every weekend for several months prior to hitting the AT (during summer in the southern hemisphere).

Whatever you do, do something. I'm a firm believer that any preparation is better than none.

As for mental preparation, and the second question I raised about backpacking experience, consider that after the first month you will still have most of the trail to go and the main problems you will run into are no longer physical. Therefore, even more preparation should be made for these inevitable mental hurdles. The best practice is gaining experience and confidence with the gear you choose to bring along. Each of these factors deserves their own discussion, but take this wisdom to heart:

> *"The more time you spend in the woods, the greater your connection to the natural world becomes. Slowly but surely you make the transition from stranger to guest to partner. And in so doing, potentially spending months hiking and camping becomes less of a psychological challenge, and more of a confirmation or a celebration." -Cam "Swami" Honan, Is thru-hiking really 90% mental?*

● ● ●

In an excellent article that is worth reading in its entirety, Spirit Eagle poses several important questions that every potential thru-hiker should ask themselves. I want to ask several similar questions here and address each of them.

How long do you want to spend on trail? This may seem like an odd question in a book about thru-hiking, but there are many ways to complete the Appalachian Trail. The two major categories into which most approaches fall are either a calendar-year thru or a multi-year section hike. The section hiker approach can then be further broken into countless styles differentiated by the length one stays on trail.

Determining whether to do a calendar-year thru-hike or a multi-year section hike usually comes down to a couple of factors; namely, are you able to give up your job, family, and current lifestyle for half a year or more, with the possibility of permanent lifestyle changes. These changes could be to your perspective, including changes that may be wholly incompatible with your old lifestyle. It may also be difficult or impossible to return to your same job or career, which may then require a change in living conditions or location.

Not just anyone can take six months or more to pursue such an involved adventure. For the reasons listed above, many people choose the section hiker approach instead. Some section hikers take decades to complete the trail, maybe only hiking a few weekends at a time. Others take the approach of hiking a week or more at a time. There is also the question of hiking the trail in order, either NOBO or SOBO, or hiking each section in the season which has the most beauty. I certainly see the allure of this latter option.

After having completed the trail, I would offer one main piece of advice for section hikers deciding how to complete the trail. Even though I began the trail in pretty good shape, I did not achieve trail fitness/trail legs for at least a few weeks. These first few weeks were by far the most physically challenging, and there's nothing in the world that will put you in the same shape as hiking that far every day. To this point, section hikers often find themselves struggling through the most difficult sections of the trail without trail legs, and they complete the whole trail in this relatively out of shape condition. Therefore, I would take into consideration this fact, and realize your hike will be much easier (physically) around the one month mark.

Are you willing to tolerate the hardships of long-distance hiking? Even though thru-hiking America's long trails is technically a walk in the park, it isn't a cake walk. The first month or so will probably be one of the most easy-going, exciting, and carefree times of your life. After the trail loses its novelty, often referred to as the Virginia blues, you should be prepared to deal with at least three more months of relatively monotonous walking and increasingly difficult trail conditions. I don't want to give the impression here that the trail is boring or lacks beauty, but if you're planning on constant vistas and skipping through fields of flowers, you might want to walk a different trail. Mentally preparing for this situation will give you a higher chance of completing your thru-hike successfully.

> *"Expect the worst. If after one week on the Trail you can honestly say that it is easier than you expected, then you will probably finish your journey."* -Warren Doyle, Founder of ALDHA (Appalachian Long Distance Hikers Association)

Ask yourself, what will you do when the shit inevitably hits the fan? The challenges of the early states primarily include overuse injuries as your body learns what you plan to put it through. Strained joints, pulled muscles, blisters, and painful chafing in your sensitive areas are common features of the first month. These can all be prevented or avoided with appropriate restraint on daily distances and quickly addressing any issues that arise. The vast majority of our zero days were taken in the first quarter of the trail, mostly due to rampant norovirus outbreaks the likes of which happened almost every year. You should probably plan to get that too, and know how to handle it and avoid spreading it to others.

These initial challenges eliminate the majority of thru-hiker hopefuls who leave the trail due to illness or injury. However, I believe the challenges that increase through the summer are more difficult. These include a worsening in the mosquito population, the post honeymoon slump/Virginia Blues, and difficult trail conditions including miles of rocks or mud, or both.

Another factor that you may not see coming is a lack of good food options. Lightweight trail food generally fits into a few specific categories, none of which are nutritionally well-balanced. This led us to craving fresh fruit and prepared foods when we got to town. Town costs such as these also play into another major factor that causes many to leave the trail: lack of funds. Although the trail can be hiked for very little money, most will ultimately underestimate their individual spending. A good rule of thumb is about 1,000 US dollars per month, but many factors contribute to this as I will discuss below.

How do you want to hike the trail? The common phrase "hike your own hike" is thrown around on the trail with little explanation to all its meanings. I want to talk about two of them here. First, a continuation from where I left off above – cost.

I once heard a story about a thru-hiker who carried a five gallon bucket in which he would keep excess food, and from which he would bathe and wash his clothes. He was avoiding towns as much as possible, and claimed to have completed the entire Appalachian Trail for less than $1,500. Others take a very different approach, staying at hostels and hotels every few days, and eating as much restaurant food as they can during their frequent trips to town. These hikers might spend upwards of $10,000 to complete the trail. Most people will find themselves somewhere in between.

Chilly and I spent around $5,000 each. We spent more money than either of us have planned primarily due to our relationship: private rooms, more showers and laundry than I intended, and adventures to both DC and New York. Regardless of your approach, your expenses will increase proportional to your time spent in town. Keep this in mind, and realize another major expense will be gear replacements or upgrades as you're exposed to the multitude of options from other thru-hikers. I would recommend having at least 50% more cash than you expect to use before seriously planning a thru-hike. Without that, you risk becoming one of the 75% who attempt the trail but don't finish.

The second major thing to address here is a question of self-imposed rules. Specifically, how much of the actual Appalachian Trail do you plan to walk?

> *"If your goal is to walk the entire Appalachian Trail, then do it. People who take shortcuts do so because they are usually shorter, quicker, or easier. So where is the challenge and honor in that? We have enough of this in the real world." -Warren Doyle, Founder of ALDHA*

This might be a little harsh, but it makes a good point. This is how Chilly and I hiked the AT, we made sure to walk past every single white blaze on the entire trail. Doing so is often called taking a "purist" approach, and fulfills the requirement to join the 2000-Miler Club (sponsored by the Appalachian Trail Conservancy). However, purism isn't the only way to hike the trail. Consider for a moment the Continental Divide Trail which has numerous accepted alternate routes and remains technically unfinished at the time of this writing. Purism does not exist for that trail, and by extension, nor does the Triple Crown. Therefore, I believe you should absolutely hike the trail how you want to hike it and not use my story or any other person or organization to determine how you do it. That being said, there are a few things to consider.

The primary non-purist way to hike the trail is blue blazing, i.e. taking alternate routes to either avoid difficult sections or to take in additional sights along the main trail. Another way to alter a purist hike is to slackpack, or have someone else transport the majority of your gear ahead for you so that you may hike with less weight. Given that this almost always costs money, I really don't know why you wouldn't just go ultralight instead and always carry weight like a slackpacker, but to each their own. Finally, there is the uncommon, and often frowned upon method of yellow-blazing defined by using cars or hitchhiking to skip sections of the trail. So how much does purism on the Appalachian Trail matter? I don't know, hike your own hike. But I will leave you with this quote for your consideration:

> "...if you start by blue-blazing Blood Mountain because you're afraid of wet rocks, what will you do on Albert Mt. in the snow? Or on Moosilauke in the fog and rain? Or on an ice-coated Katahdin? Those are some of the best parts of the Trail – will you feel the same sense of pride if you don't face the harder challenges? That's not my call – but it's something to think about." -Spirit Eagle

Are you willing to accept the possibility that your perspectives and goals could change in a way that is incompatible with your current lifestyle? As I mentioned above, an endeavor such as this always has the possibility of inducing personal change. In fact, many of those who step foot on the trail state this very purpose as their reason for hiking.

I recently performed a quick poll in a social media group for thru-hikers planning to start in the next season, specifically asking for those with no thru-hiking experience to pick from a number of categories regarding their hopes for personal change on the trail. When asked to choose between categories such as "I am hopeful that my life will change after the trail" or "I am worried that my life will change after the trail" or "I do not expect any life changes after the trail", the overwhelming majority not only expected changes to happen but were hopeful about the outcomes.

Obviously, it's a good thing that people are hopeful about their futures. I don't think many would argue otherwise. However, I wonder how many contemplate what the change would look like and how it would impact their current way of life in a practical sense. I tend to believe, given what I have read and heard from the broader thru-hiking community, that most expect a somewhat subtle change in perspective. For example, people might expect a reduction in stress or a change from pessimistic to optimistic perspective. These two in particular are reasonable expectations during the time on the trail, but once removed from that setting will they continue? What about changes that are less subtle, such as your relationship to work or your new-found addiction to endorphins in quantities that can only be found by hiking up mountains every day?

What I find particularly fascinating is how the views of these soon-to-be thru-hikers compare to the opinions of successful thru-hikers one year removed from the trail. I performed another poll in a social media group that was specifically for 2019 Appalachian Trail thru-hikers using similar questions to those asked in the other group. The response "adjusting to life after my thru-hike was difficult or involved negative outcomes" was chosen twice as often as "adjusting to life after my thru-hike was easy or involved positive outcomes". Further, though more people said their life returned to normal than said there were positive outcomes, the most frequently chosen option by far was "all I want to do is hike now". Take this initial finding with a grain of salt, we need far more data to make solid conclusions. But it's still worth considering...

The difference in the views between thru-hikers who had yet to complete the trail and those who had finished it recently is striking, and notably more negative after the hike. Interestingly, this pattern followed my own thinking too. This abundant hopefulness makes sense given the pervading narrative surrounding the trail. That is, that the great outdoors is THE source of unquestionably positive experiences and that hiking a long trail must certainly have only the best outcomes. In fact, I think this is accurate and true, but at the same time, quite misleading. Even the best and greatest personal change, even when it results from wonderful experiences in the great outdoors, can itself be a source of difficulty.

This is the topic of Appendix A; but, I want to end this section with a hopeful note and a warning. Thru-hiking will likely be one of the best experiences of your life, and it will change almost everyone who does it. I believe all of this is essentially good, but you should be prepared for the possibility that negative practical outcomes can result from unquestionably favorable personal changes. In particular, when it comes to reintegrating with broader society.

Lastly, in your preparation for the trail, remember the wisdom of going outside and putting in the miles:

> *"The world is not in your books and maps, it's out there"* -Gandalf, The Hobbit

Perspective

> *"When you unconditionally enjoy backpacking, the inevitable challenges that one encounters during a thru-hike – boredom, loneliness, physical discomfort, dodgy weather – are usually blips rather than potential reasons to quit your hike... when you enjoy something unconditionally – you are in for the long haul. The "novelty" doesn't wear off after a few weeks or a couple of months. As a result, you are always looking to improve and grow as a hiker."* –Cam "Swami" Honan

The primary mental preparations you should make prior to the trail, other than gaining trail experience, are really just a matter of perspective. They generally fall into two categories: 1, setting expectations and 2. how to keep going on the hard days. Let's start with expectations, including debunking some misconceptions about the trail as well as goal setting and planning for your thru-hike.

Setting expectations is difficult with a trail that is awash in romantic ideals, escapism, and people with a range of ability and fitness levels all hitting the trail. One hiker may tell you the next mountain is incredibly difficult, but you trained in these hills all your life so you skip all the way up like a mountain goat. Maybe you are having a rough day out there and the next hiker you see tells you camp is just one hour ahead – except they are hiking at 4mph while you are happy to get 1mph. I saw these types of situations frequently on the trail.

What caught me off guard were the range of misconceptions, or even misinformation, regarding specific sections of trail. For example, many claim that Virginia is flat and Pennsylvania is full of rocks. If you, like so many thru-hikers, reach Virginia expecting smooth sailing you will be sorely mistaken. Virginia is where I can remember the PUDs (pointless ups and downs) really setting in. The Virginia Triple Crown is far from pointless, it's really quite beautiful. The same can be said for the Grayson Highlands. But just wait until you get to the Virginia Roller Coaster, you will be cursing everyone who told you Virginia was flat!

As for the rocks, yes Pennsylvania has them aplenty; but only after the midway point. What you may not realize is that the Pennsylvania rocks are little more than a prelude to what you will see in every other northern state. Don't get to the end of Pennsylvania and think your days of stubbed toes and rolled ankles are over.

By the time you reach the White Mountains, you will have heard countless times how expensive this section is and how you will only be able to stay in the huts if you do work-for-stay. While this is an option, it turns out that the Whites can be completed for little more than $25, as opposed to the $100/night the huts generally charge. I detailed this more in the narrative section of the book so I won't rehash it all here. Suffice it to say that if you stay at an AMC official campsite early you will collect a thru-hiker ticket which will let you stay at other AMC campsites and get free food at the huts. If/when you do need to sleep at a hut, given that stealth camping is illegal and you will likely want to stay at Lake of the Clouds so you can summit Mount Washington early, you can pay $10 to sleep on the floor.

● ● ●

The small picture issues I described above are hopefully useful, but they won't make or break your hike. However, being wrong about enough of these big picture issues could send you packing.

First, ask yourself not only why you want to thru-hike; but

why, of all the trails, you want to thru-hike the AT. Now I haven't done any other long trail, but I have learned a lot about each from those who have – including Chilly who has completed both the Pacific Crest Trail (PCT) and Te Araroa (TA). What I have come to realize is that each trail has its own personality of sorts, which comes with associated strengths and weaknesses. The PCT and the CDT (Continental Divide Trail) both pass through low elevation desert and high elevation mountains, so one of the main challenges on these trails is the range of gear required between the start and finish. By comparison, the AT has much lower mountains and low alpine terrain is as difficult as the environment gets. The challenge on the AT, oddly enough, is the trail's elevation change and the grade of the trail itself. Unlike both the PCT and CDT which were graded more gradually and welcome pack animals, the AT seems to delight in taking the steepest path over the hardest boulders and talus it can find.

Common wisdom holds that the CDT is hard because it's long and isolated, the PCT is easy if you can handle the different climates, and of all three it's the terrain and monotony of the AT which is the most difficult. A little ironic that the AT is both the most popular and considered the old grand-dad of long trails.

Because the AT follows low elevation mountains, the oldest range on the planet, it stays mostly below the tree line. The result is what thru-hikers refer to as "the green tunnel", which you will be walking in for days before coming out of it for a view. Don't get me wrong, the AT has stunning vistas and a wonderful array of both flora and fauna; but, somewhere around the thousand mile mark you are probably going to get a bit tired of the green tunnel. Not to worry, you will have realized by this time one of the AT's greatest strengths – the community. Given that it's the oldest long distance trail in the US, trail communities and trail angels are abundant, and the "bubble" of thru-hikers that start in the south between March and April leads to one of the richest social experiences the outdoors can offer.

Good thing too, because if you were just out here for the views you would probably be better served on one of the other long trails...

•••

The second to last thing I want is for you to get a negative impression of the trail – a successful thru-hike is considered by most who do it as one of the best things they will ever do. I'm just trying to increase your probability of success by managing expectations. The very last thing I want is for a prospective thru-hiker to be unprepared and have a bad, or unsafe, time out there. So let me quickly run through a few more pieces of information you should have going into such an adventure.

Planning and conceptualizing. Thru-hiking takes a long time, but there is a much better way to think of the trail than all at once. Every long trail is broken up into wilderness sections and resupply locations, anything from a trail town or city down to a backwoods convenience store. When you only need to plan out the next few days, the equivalent of a long weekend trip, the challenge seems much smaller. This is a common approach to handling large goals – break it up into smaller, more manageable pieces. In this way, a trail like the AT can be thought of as a series of town hopping hikes. Don't worry, Katahdin/Springer will come before you know it – no reason to concern yourself with such a monumental task every day.

Likewise, rushing through the trail or planning too far ahead is probably detrimental most of the time. Many people like to post food boxes ahead to themselves because they expect it will make things easier. What actually ends up happening is that they either 1. send too much, or a bunch of food they liked pre-trail before their tastes change or, 2. they post it somewhere that holds hours non-conducive to thru-hiking's variable schedule. Sure, you can make this work; in fact, while I never sent myself food, I did get gear replacements by mail from time to time. However, the few times I did, it was almost always a hassle and I was happy to not need to do it more. If you do want to ship anything ahead, it's probably best to send it to a hostel where you will be staying rather than a post office or other business that holds standard hours.

I would also caution against doing too much planning in any sense, odd as that sounds. The most freeing aspect of thru-hiking, in my opinion, is being completely on your own schedule and free to change plans at a moment's notice. Chilly and I almost never planned further ahead than one, maybe two, resupply locations at most. Don't waste time pre-trail deciding when you will be where, that will very likely fall apart immediately when reality of trail life sets in. I'm not saying don't prepare. I'm saying that you should let yourself let go - enjoy the freedom.

How to prepare for tough days. Now that I have discussed setting up accurate expectations for the trail, how should a thru-hiker prepare to keep moving after the challenge sets in? This is what sends most people packing.

A common suggestion among thru-hikers is to "embrace the suck".

"...you'll have to decide how you respond, and often successful hikers find comfort in "embracing the suck", which is to simply be ok with the suffering. Be mindful and present, calm and collected, and accept that this is just part of what you wanted." –Gusha, Hiker Feed

There will be many hardships one must face in this endeavor, but I think we can do better than simply surviving them – we should thrive in spite of, or even because of, the hardships. The goal should be to enjoy, rather than endure. I believe this is best achieved by 1. having a plan in place to prevent the nearly inevitable boredom, 2. understanding the importance behind "hiking your own hike" and, 3. resisting the urge to fight both yourself and the trail.

First, boredom will impact almost everyone at some point.

One can only smell the roses, or walk the green tunnel, for so many consecutive days before you start thinking about other things. In particular, thru-hikers talk about the "Virginia Blues", but I prefer to call this the death of the honeymoon phase. Either way you cut it, the novelty of hiking long distances every day loses some of its initial luster after some amount of time; on average, this happens sometime around Virginia, or one quarter of the trail. I believe the best antidote is to have secondary objectives to complete in your spare time. This may very well be the most creative time in your life, be prepared to express yourself in some way. I was a writer before I was a hiker, so I knew I would want to take a lot of notes. For this reason, I took a voice recorder as one of my luxury items and used it frequently. Other ideas might include: working on a business idea, taking time for daily meditation, using podcasts to learn something new, or learning a language.

Second, the phrase "hike your own hike" gets thrown around a lot, but it does have some wisdom to impart to the struggling thru-hiker. Everyone is seeking something different, hiking with different gear, walking different paces, and so on; you must be comfortable doing your own thing at all times, even if it means sacrificing socialization with particular hikers. There will always be someone out there who is more similar to you than the person who is simply a bad match for your style. Feel free to go your own pace, or take that extra zero if it will keep you on the trail. This also ties into the third point which is stated quite well in this quote by Warren Doyle, Founder of ALDHA (Appalachian Long Distance Hikers Association):

> "Don't fight the Trail. You have to flow with it, be cooperative with the Trail, neither competitive nor combative."

This means you should do what you need to do at all times. If you are having a really rough time on trail, there is almost always something you can do to fix it. Don't give up, put in the time and effort to figure it out, get through it, and then enjoy your success in overcoming the near failure.

Lastly, don't fight the urge to take zero days as a means to working out any issues or ailments, or do it just because you feel like it. This is one thing Chilly and I wish we would have done better. We had very few days of actually doing nothing on our "days off", we would always find some way to do something active and fail to give our bodies the much needed and well deserved rest. When you need a zero, take a real zero – it will make the days that follow all the more productive.

And always remember, never quit on a bad day.

Gear

"The more I carry the more I like camping, the less I carry the more I like hiking." –Unknown

Gear choices often fall into the category of "hike your own hike", and there is rarely a one size fits all type of answer. That being said, I want to share what has worked best for me after years of trial and error. Here are a few guidelines worth mentioning that will help people with packs in all weight ranges.

1. Less is more. A lighter pack is more comfortable and will reduce your chance of injury.
2. Try to keep the "big 3" under 2 pounds each. Big 3 = tent, pack, and sleeping system.
3. Each piece of gear should serve as many purposes as possible.

Packs. Always buy your pack last, or at least wait until you are certain what will be going in it. What you want to avoid is buying a pack that is too big, empty spaces will generally be filled whether you need those extra items or not. In 2019 I used two packs on the trail, both of them were great for a specific range of pack weights. If your total pack weight is more than 20 pounds, I like the Osprey Exos 48 liter pack. The Exos is considered a great entry level pack for lightweight backpacking and I would recommend it to anyone. Osprey also has their "Almighty Guarantee" in case you run into any trouble with the pack.

Once I began dropping pack weight, eventually settling at a base weight of 7.5 pounds, I did a lot more research on packs for the weight range under 20 pounds. I wanted to go without a hip belt because I was getting bruises from mine, and they are really hot during the summer months. Instead of the hip belt, I decided on a running vest style harness to help with weight distribution. The best pack in this category in 2019, in my opinion, was the Nashville Pack and Equipment Company "Cutaway". They are a new cottage company with great customer service, and their pack is about as light as anything on the market at 12oz. This pack carries very comfortably with total pack weights below 20 pounds, and especially shines below 15. There are more and more pack options in this category each year, so I will leave you with this last piece of advice: always look at the cottage companies before going with the pack that everyone else has, you will save a significant amount of money, weight (sometimes), and headaches if you have to deal with customer service.

Pack organization. Many backpackers fall into the two extremes when organizing their packs: either not at all, or drybags for everything including a drybag for all their drybags. Let me save you a shakedown or two by sharing with you how I think about pack organization.

Ultimately, you have two groups of items – things that will get wet at some point, and things that can't ever get wet. Your pack itself falls into the first category even if you like having a rain cover. The problem with rain covers is that they are imperfect, the weak point at the back of the cover will allow either rain or sweat to soak the pack at some point.

So what is a backpacker to do? I suggest letting the things that will get wet stay unprotected from rain. Leave that pack cover at home. Instead, use a pack liner. This can be as simple as a black garbage bag/compactor bag, or as nice as a 50L drybag that may cost you a pretty penny. This pack liner is for your sleeping system, your down jacket and any spare clothing, and anything else that needs to stay dry and won't be needed throughout the day. An optional, smaller dry bag could be used for things that you want inside the pack liner but may themselves be wet such as a toothbrush, contact lens case, etc. Anything that you need for the day can go in a third dry bag and this can sit in your pack on top of the pack liner, tent, raincoat, etc. My food bags are also waterproof and stay outside the pack liner (they also warrant a separate discussion). That's it, you can probably leave any other drybags and stuff sacks at home, including those for your sleeping bag and pad. Remember, bags add weight too; but they also add effort every time you make or break camp.

I also became quite partial to the fanny pack lifestyle early in the trail. Of course, you are going to look a bit foolish wearing a fanny pack; but in 2019, fanny packs were all the rage with thru-hikers, and it's easy to see why. First, it puts a few useful items in a central location for use during the day. I keep my phone, headphones, and snacks in the fanny pack. Second, it allows you to redistribute some weight off your back and place it closer to your center of gravity. You could take this to the next level and get a front pack, but hopefully you don't have enough stuff to go that far. Third, if you purchase a "waterproof" model like the one I used (Northface Bozer 2L) you won't need to worry about protecting your phone/camera that you may be using many times a day. I highly recommend trying this out; don't worry, thru-hikers don't judge!

Clothing and layers. When thinking about clothing, there are the two critical aspects to consider: layering, and removing redundancies. Layering is the key to keeping warm in the wilderness. For the AT, starting in spring and ending before winter, you will need three essential layers at all times and one extra layer for the coldest sections of the trail (including both the Smoky Mountains and the White Mountains). The first layer is a base, usually either Merino wool or a synthetic polyester blend. I used a synthetic base layer top and leggings (instead of underwear, though underwear in either material is more common). I also wore lightweight hiking shorts so I had pockets (and could cover up a little more in public, no one wants to see that). The second layer is for warmth, either a down or synthetic puffy jacket or a lightweight fleece. The optional layer will be the other of these two, whichever is not in your standard kit. Personally, I would make the fleece standard since it does better when wet and can be more easily cleaned.

The final, outside layer is a rain shell. This is a source of some contention; but let me simplify this decision for you. If you are hiking up mountains in the rain, you are going to get soaked by either the rain or by sweat. A fancy $400 rain shell isn't going to prevent that. Go with something cheap, light, and comfortable instead. I went with the $20 Frogg Togg Ultralight 2 rain suit – available everywhere, and replaced easily.

None of these individual layers need account for much individual warmth, but together they will keep you toasty even in high winds or rain.

The other key concept when packing your clothing is to remove redundant copies. I have seen thru-hikers start the AT with ten changes of clothes, expecting to switch into a clean set each day. Just this level of overpacking alone would require a bigger, more expensive pack, and would weigh more than any ultralight kit. Some prospective thru-hikers worry about their smell on the trail, or keeping clean in general; this seems to be the root cause of overpacking clothes.

Flip that thinking on its head. Day-hikers all walk around

smelling like the poster children for Brand X deodorant, or whatever laundry detergent they use. At first you may think it smells pleasant, but the more I smelled it the more repulsive I found it – no one smells natural, and all the smells are really quite overpowering once you are no longer desensitized to it. Our recent ancestors didn't wash but once a month, you can get by on once a week for the duration of a thru-hike.

The only item you need two copies of are your socks, to help keep your feet dry and to double up on cold nights. Other than that, just one of each layer will be fine. You will have an opportunity to do laundry about twice a week if you choose, and you can always rinse your clothes out with running water (don't use soap in rivers, of course, just rinse out the salt).

An extra consideration for thru-hikers is something to wear on laundry day, or around town in general. I picked up a pair of lightweight laundry shorts (from Dutchware Gear), and either wore my puffy or rain jacket on top. Chilly carried a lightweight dress. Many hostels have loaner clothes for just this reason, but don't get caught needing to do laundry and having nothing to wear!

Feet. As mentioned above, two pairs of socks is standard practice in the backcountry. The exact type of socks will vary depending on your shoe choice.

I wore hiking boots years ago, but long since switched to trail runners for two main reasons: 1. your feet will get wet either way, shoes will dry much faster than boots and, 2. shoes are much lighter, and as the saying goes "one pound on the feet equals five in the pack".

That being said, hike your own hike. If you wear boots, I would recommend using a sock liner inside of a wool sock. This both wicks away sweat and places friction between the two socks rather than on your feet, both of which will help prevent blisters. If you wear trail runners, I recommend looking into toe socks

(I used Injinji brand). These will likewise prevent blisters between, or on, toes. I've not had blister problems on my heels in trail runners.

Hats vs. hoods. The AT will expose you to an abundance of both rain and sun, you would be wise to carry some head protection. I tend to carry a rather unique hat for North America, you may have noticed if you have seen my hiking photos (or looked at the back cover of this book). After trying many different options, I settled on the rice paddy hat for a few reasons – even if you don't like my hat choice you may find similar qualities in other hats.

The rice paddy hat is very wide and protects my neck from the sun while doing an equally great job in the rain. When the rain comes down hard, having such a hat provides a wide area of dry space near my face – this is why I prefer a hat over a hood, which by comparison, can feel oppressive in the rain. I also tend to hike trails that are overgrown, so having some structure helps protect my head from small branches and vines. I prefer a hat made from natural materials to provide this structure, but a similar style hat also comes in synthetic materials from companies like Kavu.

Trekking poles. Whether or not you use trekking poles will often depend on the style tent you choose, but I decided I liked them when I was still using free standing tents. More than once my trekking poles have stopped me from rolling down hills, or have caught my weight before I roll an ankle. When used properly, they make both uphill and downhill easier on the muscles and joints respectively – a huge benefit when you have a bad knee like I do. Chilly started the AT with poles, but used them less and less as time went on, and ended up sending them home from around the halfway point.

I only have two pieces of advice for poles: get a set with cork handles, they retain their grip and comfort better in wet conditions, and use poles with lever locks as they are easiest to use in all weather conditions and are far less likely to fail than the twist lock version.

Water. You will definitely want some kind of water purification system on the AT where both road contamination and Giardia are common. The current water purification options force hikers to choose between speed, taste, and weight – you can only have two of the three it seems. There are also three major types of water purification used in backpacking: chemical solutions, size exclusion filters, and carbon filters.

For the best taste, you will want one of the many carbon filters which removes impurities like heavy metals in addition to size excluding bacteria and viruses. Unfortunately, this style filter has remained bulky and much heavier than the other two options which are, therefore, more common on the AT.

Chemical purification comes in various forms and kills organic impurities like bacteria and viruses, but it leaves metals and other bad tastes. I don't care for this method personally, but some people use it as a backup in case their main filter breaks.

The most common method, with both speed and low weight, is size exclusion. The most popular filters in this category are the Sawyer and the Katadyn BeFree. I began the trail with a Sawyer, but immediately switched after seeing the flow rate of the BeFree. One thing to keep in mind with size exclusion filters is that heavy metals are not removed; therefore, you should gather your water close to the source if possible, and always far away from road runoff.

Food. To hang or not to hang? Bear canister, or use your food as a pillow? What to do with your food is probably a source of many questions, or at least some level of concern. It's also a hotly debated topic even among forestry departments, not to mention hikers themselves.

Even as I write, the forestry service is working on mandating bear cans for North Carolina. Georgia has been talking about it for years. While thru-hiking, my group of friends and I were often lectured by officials of various types about using the bear boxes they provide, or bear wire, or hanging your food at night – almost to the point of fear mongering at times. I understand the concern, and the fact that bears must be euthanized if they become too drawn to humans. But let's look at the facts.

First, you will be dealing with black bears on the AT. On a trail like the CDT, where you will be in grizzly country for portions of the trip, you will want to keep your food far away from you, and a bear canister is highly recommended. However, as we're talking about the AT, let's focus on black bears.

Black bears kill less than one person per year on average; in fact, you are more likely to die of lightning or bees (https://bear.org/how-dangerous-are-black-bears/). Including all bear species, there are only an average of forty bear attacks each year around the world (https://petpedia.co/bear-attack-statistics/). The reality is that back bears generally avoid people unless those people come near the cubs. This means they will generally avoid campsites as well.

Sure, we all know people with stories of bears coming to their campsites, and rangers will tell you theirs without being prompted. You may have a story yourself; but, what is the main factor attracting animals to humans?

Both bears and mice, the latter a much more common problem for overnight hikers as they will eat through your pack or tent to find the crumbs you forgot to clean up, are attracted to food primarily by the sense of smell. It would seem obvious that any method which doesn't prevent smell from traveling is still inviting bears and mice to the food, and thus, is an inferior method of prevention. Even so, none of the recommended methods for food protection include scent proofing. This includes bear canisters, bear boxes, and every form of hanging. This is despite the fact that such methods not only exist, but they can (and should) be combined with whatever other method you choose.

The best method of keeping animals away from your food is to use scent proof bags. The Opsak bags made by Loksak were the scent proofing option of choice by myself and countless other hikers in 2019.

Even in the year of this writing, when superior methods exist, the top forestry agents are still debating the use of outdated technology despite the fact that it doesn't prevent or discourage bear encounters at the food storage site. They are still teaching bag hanging methods, and spending taxpayer money, or donations, to build bear boxes and wires near campsites. They certainly mean well, but the outdoor community can do better with updated technology. Do your part to keep bears out of campsites by using scent proofing methods, either by themselves or in combinations with the other, more conventional methods.

Bug repellant. Spring and summer in the Eastern United States requires protection from two bugs in particular: ticks and mosquitoes. Both of these insects carry an assortment of parasites and/or diseases which you very much want to avoid. Some will leave an infected person with disabilities lasting months or years.

At one point on the trail, the mosquitoes and other flying insects were so thick that I was wearing sunglasses to protect my eyes, even at dusk. We tried every trick in the books to prevent mosquitoes, but found DEET was by far the best. Of course, you don't want to use DEET if you don't have to – it's absorbed into the bloodstream, and it destroys synthetic materials. However, we still found that mosquitoes would find any tiny patch of skin that wasn't covered in the chemicals. The other sprays, such as picaridin, sometimes worked for a while; but none lasted long once we started to sweat.

The other layer of protection from bugs, specifically ticks, is permethrin treatment of clothing. This is a chemical wash that can be found online and through outdoor retailers. It claims to last for seven washes; but seems to count hard rains as well. This does work well enough for a while, but will require multiple treatments during a thru-hike. The other tip that no thru-hiker wants to hear is this: wearing long sleeves and pants will be the best defense, but remember that mosquitoes can still bite through thin clothing.

What to leave behind. A common question in hiking groups is about what should be left behind. First and foremost, leave behind your fears. They say you pack your fears, or in other words, more fear leads to packing more gear you don't need. Go get some experience and learn what you do and don't need, then try to pack less as you become more experienced.

As for specific items to ditch, I would start with bear mace. Black bears are much more afraid of you than you are of them and will run away if you make loud noises. Just be sure to stay away from their cubs. Likewise, leave your firearm at home; you won't ever have the need and it will only serve to make your fellow thru-hikers uneasy.

You can also leave your camping chair at home. If you don't like the idea of sitting on cold rock, instead bring a Z-Seat which weighs only two ounces and packs much better than a chair. I also found that camp shoes were unnecessary. I started the trail with down booties, which were certainly nice in the cold spring. Eventually, I just became accustomed to walking around camp barefoot. Now I prefer being barefoot during ever season except winter.

Practical Ultralighting. When preparing for a backpacking trip, people tend to think of the essentials first. The problem is that almost no one can agree on what is actually essential. Many traditional backpackers will agree with a list that looks like this one from "Backpacking with the Saints" by Belden Lane:

"Map • Compass (or GPS) • Flashlight or headlamp • Food • Water (with purification tablets or filter for backcountry water sites) • Extra clothing (including rain gear) • First-aid kit (with sunscreen lotion) • Matches and firestarter (a cheap butane lighter) • Pocket knife • Basic survival kit (emergency moon blanket, signal mirror, whistle, and 8×8-inch square of heavy-duty aluminum foil for makeshift cookpot)"

More spartan backpacks will find Henry David Thoreau's list on the necessities of life more applicable: food, shelter, clothing, and fuel. In fact, if you added to that list a pack in which to store the rest, you could thru-hike the AT with nothing more, and you could even leave that fuel at home.

Now that I have demonstrated my disclaimer, i.e. that someone who reads this will certainly disagree with what I'm about to say, let me tell you how little you actually need to hike the whole trail:

1. Shelter
2. Clothing and raingear
3. Sleep system
4. Food and Water
5. Pack (buy this last, get the smallest one into which you can fit 1-4)

Everything else is a luxury. The difference in this list and most lists is merely a matter of trail confidence, the knowledge required to solve problems, and a willingness to compromise on certain comforts. Even so, we all make a few compromises; but, when designing a kit you should start with these items, and get the lightest you can find.

Before going further, let me give you a standard definition of the backpacking "weight classes" (the traditional class is anything above that which is listed; base weight = pack weight minus consumables):

- Lightweight: Base weight under 20 pounds. Goal: Big 3 less than 10 pounds together
- Ultralight: Base weight under 10 pounds. Goal: Big 3 less than 6 pounds together
- Super-ultralight: Base weight under 5 pounds. Goal: Big 3 less than 3 pounds together

I want to emphasize that these cutoffs are both arbitrary and, importantly, the agreed upon guidelines for discussing pack weights and backpacking philosophy within the ultralight community. It should not be taken so seriously as to care about being exactly under ten pounds. Just for ease of discussion, I will use these guidelines here.

The general rule of thumb in the ultralight community is that each of your "Big Three" (tent, pack, sleeping system) should weigh less than two pounds. This gives a solid base from which to build your kit, knowing then that everything else together should weigh less than four pounds. After this point, the key is to dramatically limit what you add to the kit.

Although a trail like the AT, with its frequent blazing and countless trail signs, requires no map or compass, most will carry some form of wayfinding equipment. In fact, a smart phone is probably the sixth item on most people's list because it works for navigation and so much more. Another item many want, myself included, is an inflatable pillow.

Further progress in reducing base weight often involves switching from tents to tarps, or using some homemade gear; but neither is required.

Many will be concerned about the price of ultralight gear, but there are plenty of Big Three items that weight under two pounds and are relatively inexpensive. You can make an ultralight kit with store bought gear for less than $1000. You can reduce this further by making some of your own gear. If you are interested in this route, check out the "MYOG" (make your own gear) community on Reddit to get started.

I'm absolutely certain that the gear will only get better and cheaper as time goes on.

Since the goal of this section is to challenge your idea of what is "essential", consider tossing out your stove, fuel, and cookware as well. Doing so will save you time and effort in both food prep and clean up. It also rids your pack of several hard edged items that can poke you in the back.

Personally, I cold soak my food in a Ziploc bag. Many common hiker foods such as ramen and instant potatoes, or several other pastas, are ready in just twenty to thirty minutes. I don't even use utensils – just eat it straight from the bag. This saves time and energy, in addition to weight and space. It also gives your travel companions a good laugh from time to time.

> *"Leave your cultural 'level of comfort' at home. Reduce your material wants while concentrating on your physical and spiritual needs." –Warren Doyle*

In the 60's, the well-known gear maker Kelty suggested that a good pack weight was between 17 and 25 pounds. This might make you think everyone could easily be ultralight nowadays, and I even suggested to Chilly that for that weight I would be swimming in luxury nowadays. But, that won't necessarily hold true for everyone. Each person will have a different level of comfort they expect, and some conditions will require packing more gear. This is why it's critically important to think about ultralight backpacking as a secondary benefit, or icing on the cake; but the cake itself is minimalism. Minimalism helps to loosen attachment to material possessions, and experience freedom rather than fear in the wilderness away from the comforts of modern conveniences.

Having said that, I won't deny that carrying less weight leads to more smiles and more miles! I think back to the weariness and woe described by Bill Bryson, crushed beneath traditional gear; by comparison I bounded up the mountain, practically skipping with joy and a lightheartedness that lifted my pack like the helium in party balloons.

Even if you are currently a traditional backpacker, I would urge you to give this approach a shot, even if it's just one night in the backcountry. The benefits of shedding any amount of weight are countless; but, getting anywhere near ultralight will provide you with both a safer and more enjoyable backpacking experience.

Etiquette

Just as in any social setting, there are a few behavioral guidelines hikers should follow in the woods. I'm not writing this section to act as the etiquette police; on the contrary, I'm letting you know what will make you despised by your fellow hikers so that you can avoid it.

Trail. The trail is a place of freedom where everyone can hike their own hike, enjoy the sights and sounds of nature, or express themselves in almost any way. The line is drawn where it's always drawn, the point where your freedom interferes with the freedom of others to enjoy the trail their own way. The two primary behaviors to avoid are continuous loud noises, such as music through speakers, and failure to leave no trace (LNT). This failure to LNT shows up in ways that range from annoying, such as food crumbs dropped on trail (I'm sure we have all been guilty of this), to the disgusting inability to properly dispose of human waste and toilet paper which ends up being blown around by the wind.

Leave no trace. LNT is a simple set of guidelines whose goal is minimal impact to natural environments for the benefit of all: animal, plant, or fungi. These guidelines are always open to change as new information comes to light regarding what is, or is not, considered good practice. Therefore, don't get so set in your ways as to not be open to change, and always do your best to follow LNT principles.

The most important, entry level understanding of LNT suggests that you should leave nature where you found it, take your rubbish with you when you leave, and don't impact animals or natural environments with fires or any other practices. I like to believe that most people take these principles to heart, but their methods are not sufficient to prevent impact. I want to talk about three categories in which I saw issues far too often on the trail:

1. Poop. Catholes should be dug 200 feet away from water sources, the trail, and any possible campsites. Holes should be dug 6-8 inches deep, 4-6 inches wide in soil with as few rocks and roots as possible. The depth should be slightly shallower in sand to allow for better decomposition. Holes can be dug with trowels, sticks, trekking poles, or rocks; just make sure the depth is correct. The only things that go in the cat hole are feces and biodegradable toilet paper; not wipes or towels, not cloth, not trash. Cover the hole with soil and leaves, at least two inches deep. Do not use rocks and sticks. All of this is extremely important to keeping the trail clean, and to allow for proper biodegradation. Do anything less and you risk having your toilet paper blown onto the trail or dug up animals.

2. Cleaning. Pots, utensils, and other cookware should be

rinsed with water in the outback, save the soap for town. At the time of this writing, no "eco-safe" soaps are actually safe to use in the woods without harming wildlife. This isn't likely to change given what's required to kill bacteria. For pots that are especially dirty, water can be boiled until clean. For disposal, it should either be drunk or dispersed over a wide area away from campsites and shelters. Dispersing the water makes it so a single space is not a clearly attractive location for wildlife to lick. People following the strictest LNT principles will just drink their waste water. Toothpaste should likewise be packed out (spit into a trash bag), but can also be dispersed like cleaning water. I would highly encourage you to just pack it out; but rangers were still telling hikers dispersing it was OK in 2019.

3. Garbage. All garbage should be packed out. The only exception is toilet paper, which should be buried properly. Even things that appear "natural" or biodegradable, such as fruit waste, should be packed out. Banana peels and orange rinds are particularly dangerous to wildlife. Orange rinds hold water for much longer than other such waste and can spoil a squirrel's entire stockpile of winter food. Seeds from various fruits are also problematic if they not native to the area. Don't even question it, just pack it out.

"There are people who 'hike' through life. They measure life in terms of money and amusement; they rush along the trail of life feverishly seeking to make a dollar or gratify an appetite. How much better to "saunter" along this trail of life, to measure it in terms of beauty and love and friendship! How much finer to take time to know and understand the men and women along the way, to stop a while and let the beauty of the sunset possess the soul, to listen to what the trees are saying and the songs of the birds, and to gather the fragrant little flowers

that bloom all along the trail of life for those who have eyes to see!" –Albert Palmer, The Mountain and Its Message 1911

I would urge you to heed Mr. Palmer's words while minding modern Leave No Trace Principles, gathering the flowers in photographs only.

More information can be found at: *lnt.org*

Camp. Many campsites on the AT have space for multiple tents and hammocks. These shared campsites will generally have obvious places for hanging food bags; regardless, if you are hanging your food, you should do so far away from both yourself and other campers. On my own thru-hike, I saw bear hangs immediately beside tents far too often – sometimes the food didn't even belong with the people in that tent!

The other norm you will quickly discover is that of "hiker midnight". This happens at sundown and is the time most thru-hikers will be in their tents, trying to sleep. You will find the scorn of trail weary thru-hikers if you brazenly ignore hiker midnight either on trail, or in hostels. On a similar note, use only the red light setting on your headlamp in any and all shared spaces after the sun goes down. The red wavelength will prevent your nightly bladder voiding run from waking up a shelter full of grumpy hikers.

Shelters, hostels, and hiker boxes. What you should keep in mind at these locations is very similar to the shared campsite with one major difference. Shelters and hostels, as well as some trail shops and churches, will have hiker boxes. These are "take an item, leave an item" style boxes in which hikers donate gear they no longer need. Sometimes, there are also boxes for food. These boxes are always like a treasure hunt in which you may just provide something useful, fun, or tasty. But, what you should never do is use these boxes as trash bins. Foods should be unopened, not homemade, and not outdated. Likewise, gear should be in good condition – if it's trash, put it in the trash can.

Party culture. People hike the AT for many reasons. Some start the trail just after graduating and see it as a last hurrah before settling down. Others take an opposite approach of using a thru-hike to rid themselves of the burdens of addiction. These two groups may be concerned about the other, and attempt to avoid an uneasy encounter. My disclaimer here is that I don't belong to either of these groups, but will share with you what I experienced.

If the plan for your thru-hike involves mind altering substances, you will find them; and with them you will find a group of people looking to enjoy themselves in that way. If, on the other hand, you are seeking complete abstinence, then you can find both a space for it and a group of like-minded individuals. Without purposefully seeking or avoiding such things, I was able to see that either path was readily available. As they say, the trail provides.

Health

Nutrition. Thru-hikers will require somewhere between two and three times as many calories as they needed off trail just to maintain their body weight. What this means, in practice, is that thru-hikers end up eating a lot of junk food high in fats and sugars just to keep up. To keep our pack weight in check, we tried to bring food that has high calorie density and aimed to stay above 100 calories per ounce for each item.

One piece of advice I would offer is that thru-hikers should eat what they want, not what they think they should eat. This is the only way you will get enough calories. For people this active, you won't gain weight but you certainly wouldn't eat like this forever without risking diabetes and severe vitamin deficiencies. In the short term, it's this nutritional deficit which you will quickly recognize. To prevent these deficiencies, we found that eating fresh fruits and vegetables whenever we were in town was not only helpful, but often it was a craving. In addition, carrying and taking a multivitamin will help round out your nutritional needs.

Beyond these concerns, you will also be depleting your electrolyte levels on a daily basis, and will need a salt replacement strategy else you risk developing muscle cramps and headaches. For this purpose, we found Propel drink mix packets were compact and delivered exactly what we needed. For those who need a caffeine boost as well, Walmart carries a store brand drink mix packet containing both electrolytes and caffeine.

Skin care. Chafing and hotspot are the main issues in this category, though I also had issues with dryness in my beard and on my elbows. Chafing comes mostly from sweat salts which are rubbed between moving body parts. For this problem, washing in a river does wonders. Chaffing can also be cleared up by using your hand sanitizer. I find that the hand sanitizer and river water approach is a less disgusting way to handle these problems than Body Glide, but that is the more common alternative.

For any and all hotspots, blisters, cuts, etc. – Leukotape is the best answer I have found, and I have tried it all. Many will use duct tape, but this can irritate the skin of some people; if your skin can tolerate it, and you don't mind the residue, it will work fine. Other medical tapes never seem to stick long enough to solve the problem. Leukotape, on the other hand, will generally stay on until you remove it and just a single layer is usually enough to prevent hotspots from turning into blisters. If you are like me, your feet will probably be covered in this stuff at the beginning of the trail. Although I wrote about toe socks in the gear section, I just want to reference them again here as a great preventative for toe blisters – I've never had any since switching.

I also found that dry skin became a real problem as my beard grew longer. In pre-trail life, Head and Shoulders shampoo or beard oil would prevent this; but on the trail it became painful. I eventually started carrying a travel sized lotion (but I should have found a travel size Head and Shoulders instead). Chilly had trouble with foot dryness and cracking. Her solution to the problem was O'Keeffe's Healthy Feet foot cream, and it works wonders on all sorts of skin dryness. Try to head these problems off early, before they are impossible to fight back.

Illness prevention. The primary illness you will deal with (in the pre-Covid 19 world), either directly or indirectly, is the norovirus. Many, or even most, thru-hikers get it if they hike in the NOBO bubble. We both did, despite being careful. Prevention methods include not sharing food, not touching other hikers, and keeping your hands clean. It's passed primarily through particles coming from bodily fluids. If you do get it, know that you are in for two to five days of frequent vomiting and diarrhea. You should isolate yourself from other hikers and the places they go, stay out of hostels and shelters in particular, and make sure to have a water source nearby – staying hydrated is the best thing you can do at this point. Just remember you're highly contagious. Do everything you can to prevent contaminating water sources, highly used campsites, or other shared spaces.

I'm not going to deal with Covid specifically; please follow current guidelines from the ATC/PCTA/CDTC, CDC, NIH, WHO and other governing bodies.

The other form of illness prevention will involve insect repellents which were discussed in the gear section. If you do find yourself with an attached tick there are several things to know. Ticks should be removed using tick keys or fine forceps/tweezers; grabbing by the head assuring to remove all components of the head in swift motion. Infection comes primarily from two sources, 1. remaining body components and 2. regurgitated fluids. Prevent regurgitation by not doing anything to upset the tick's sense of safety such as suffocation, chemical application, burning, or alcohol. Physical removal is the only safe method. Keep an eye on the bite location over the next few days. Lyme disease is the main worry at this point, but will not likely be transmitted if the tick is removed within 24 hours. Although not always present, a bullseye shaped redness around the bite is an indication of Lyme disease. If you think you may have Lyme, head to one of the walk-in clinics on trail – keep the tick and bring it to the doctor if at all possible.

Trail Romance

If you choose to hike with a romantic partner, or are lucky enough to find one on the trail, you will face a unique set of challenges. On one hand, the trail will make it incredibly difficult for people to hide their true selves as some might do when dating. On the other hand, you will see the good, the bad, and the ugly – both from your partner and yourself. Both of you will be presented in a more natural state, devoid of the stage act we put on in front of polite company (read: normal, non-hikers). Hikers may even find that the post-trail persona differs substantially from the person you knew on trail. Again, this will be true for both you and your partner, so some degree of compromise and acceptance should be reserved for this near inevitability.

If you are sharing a tent at any point, you will also be exposed to the hiker stench produced by working hard in the heat and dirt and not showering for a week or more at a time. The upshot here is that you will be in the best shape of your lives, brains swimming in daily endorphin highs, constantly in tune with nature, and forming bonds tighter than could be formed in years spent off trail. Needless to say, the conditions for romance are at once challenging and perfect.

Several questions should be answered along with your partner before going far together; but before I address that, I want to first discuss consensual courtship on trail; or as thru-hikers sometimes call it, pink blazing.

Pink blazing and consent. I didn't start the trail with plans of finding my future wife. On the contrary, I had explicit plans to avoid potentially romantic run-ins on trail. Not only does the trail provide, as they say, it also doesn't care about your expectations. I barely had time to sleep on the trail before my partner walked into my life. Most will not be so lucky, but many will try. The trouble arises when people, almost always men, begin to cross the line between courtship and stalking.

Specifically, pink blazing involves changing your hiking plans, pace, or using other methods to force contact between you and a potential partner. In my opinion, pink blazing walks too fine a line. It's worth noting that neither Chilly nor I believe that any pink blazing was involved in our case.

Although your advances may seem reasonable to you, extreme caution must be taken to avoid negatively impacting someone else's hike; or worse, make them feel unsafe. The trail environment causes most people to head the same direction, interact with many of the same people multiple times over many days, and be involved in trail gossip – all of which can be difficult to avoid if you need to. Err on the side of caution and respect before going over any line of no return, and always keep consent at the forefront of your mind.

One of the best ways to do this is to make your company optional. Don't make your run-ins constant or unnatural, give space for them to come to you as well. This also gives them space to let you go, a critical safety net for both parties. And whatever you do, never let yourself become a stalker. If the signals say no, then let it go.

It goes without saying that I'm no expert on women's trail experiences and feelings of safety on trail, but the last thing I want is for our story to somehow encourage bad actors. Chilly and I practiced the suggestions above on multiple occasions leading up to Standing Indian Mountain where we made it official. More than once we set out alone, but the other caught up and we camped together each night. It was organic, we each had volunteered personal details of our lives, and we had each given clear signs that we consented to the other's company. At the moment of truth, on Standing Indian, I was all but certain of the outcome given this reciprocity; however, had my advances been rejected, I would have been ready to hike on alone knowing I would find more hiking partners. I'm not holding myself up as some paragon of proper behavior, simply demonstrating how to put these concepts into practice.

What will each person do if the other needs to leave the trail early? Only about a quarter of the people who plan to finish their thru-hike of the AT actually do; so statistically, one of you won't. Now of course, if one of you completes the trail I think it's more likely that you both do. Even so, you would be wise to discuss this possibility before it happens. Decide beforehand whether or not you will continue if the other one drops out, and will you wait for them if they become injured or sick.

You may think the obvious answer to these questions is that you will do whatever they do. This is probably if you are married. However, consider the possibility that you may join a tramily which won't likely wait for a single member. Will you continue with them or stay with your friend from pre-trail? Keep in mind that your relationships with these new people will grow at a faster rate than normal relationships would given that you're probably spending 24/7 with them and sharing the glory and hardships of a grand adventure.

Another possibility to consider is that one partner may need to drop off but could rejoin later. Will they start where they left off, or skip ahead to join you? If they do the latter, will you join them when they want to return to their skipped section?

The closest situation of this type that Chilly and I encountered was catching norovirus one at a time near the beginning of the trail. Many people may not have stayed with the other while they had a contagious disease, but I think this was one of the critical moments of our relationship. This is what makes our relationship stronger than it would be if we were just friends, or just trail acquaintances. We had to make the decisions on the spot; if you're reading this, and have time to prepare, you may not have to.

What if you each hike at different paces? Hiking fast is often blamed on ego or competitive nature, but it can also be a matter of comfort. I find going slower than a certain pace really grinds my gears. Luckily, my comfort range overlaps with hers.

If the hiking paces in your group differ substantially, the common wisdom says that the fastest hikers hike in the back and allow the slowest to dictate the pace. This usually works quite well on a short weekend trip. But ask yourself, do you want to walk at a significantly slower, or faster, pace for the next five months? I will strongly suggest the answer is no. Thru-hikers will generally find that tramilies consist of hikers with substantially similar hiking paces. Of course, there are always exceptions to the rules. But, you can read countless stories of thru-hikers who left their friends behind early on the trail because of differences in either hiking speed or other preferences.

A related consideration for hiking with a partner is whether or not you will hike together during the day, or just meet up at camp. Each approach has its advantages. Hiking together during the day means that you will have a conversation partner and can decide on the fly how far you want to walk. It also provides the option to stop early in a storm, a choice you may not have if you are sharing gear.

On the other hand, hiking separately allows for quiet contemplation and walking your own pace every day (assuming the total distance you hike matches your partner's). The major downside to this approach is needing to plan a specific campsite every day. Chilly and I both agree that less planning makes for a more enjoyable adventure by allowing each day to come as it may. It wouldn't be much fun pitting your own needs against your partner's all the way up the trail.

How will you divide up the chores and gear? The degree to which you share your hike with another likely won't match Chilly and mine unless you are in a romantic relationship, but it will likely include sharing at least some of the chores some of the time. At the very least, it's common for tramilies or hiking partners to share laundry at hostels or hotels. You may also find yourselves cooking together, though this is something we rarely did. Whatever you share, you will need to decide who is responsible for what. This may include picking up the laundry, cooking and/or cleaning the dishes, or setting up and breaking down camp if you share a tent.

Once you begin sharing gear, if you ever do, you will want to make an effort towards having equal weights. What you definitely don't want to do is find yourself in a situation where you are balancing the pack weights by taking a bunch of their gear. Taking both sleeping bags and pads while they carry the tent is one thing, but taking five or more pounds of their gear is completely another. Unfair relationships happen on the trail just as they do everywhere else in life, don't let yourself get taken advantage of in the woods either. The obvious exception to this is if one person is less fit or able and a somewhat uneven weight distribution allows for the couple to work better together.

How will hiking as a couple affect others? Chilly and I began hiking together almost immediately after starting the AT; and although we had short periods of time when we hiked with one or two others, there was always some reason for our group to split up. For the majority of the trail, we hiked as a pair. To be fair, pairs were the most common number of people we saw – tramilies appear less common than both pairs and single hikers. That may undermine this point somewhat, but we wondered if we never formed a trail family because of the third wheel effect;

in other words, no one wants to hike with a romantic couple without other people around. We wondered if we got over that third wheel issue long enough, could we then form a tramily?

On the other hand, we believe that hiking as a couple brought on additional acts of kindness to which we may not have been otherwise exposed. Simply being a "cute thru-hiking couple" may have resulted in more instances of kind strangers paying for meals, or ice cream, or simply handing us cash. Each of those things happened multiple times. I'm absolutely certain that our hitchhiking experience (or mine specifically) was better in a couple than as a solo (male) hiker. I expect people think couples are less likely to be serial killers or raging lunatics.

Other couples sometimes claim that hiking together makes you more insular, less likely to engage others, and less likely to be engaged by others. The argument for this is that couples may seem more self-sufficient than single hikers. We didn't find this true for us, other than the fact that my need for socialization was often sufficiently filled by being with her rather than needing to talk to others at every shelter or campsite. This wasn't always the case however, we put in the effort to make friends and talk to plenty of other thru-hikers. Her more than I, to tell the truth.

How does affection work on the trail? Hiking with a partner will change your experience. Good partners are willing to make the hike fit the needs, speeds, and styles of both people (but most will draw the line when it negatively impacts their own hike). Hiking with a romantic partner makes this all the more true. The core feature of a good partnership is the willingness and ability to compromise; and looking back now, the lessons from the trail absolutely made compromise even easier post-trail.

One change romantic partners almost always make while hiking together is staying cleaner than they might have if hiking solo. Looking, and smelling, better than absolutely repulsive is key to a good relationship on trail as much as anywhere else. I, for one, would have showered and cleaned my clothes far less had I hiked the whole trail solo. I would have also stayed in towns less, and Chilly has said the same. The downside here is the increased cost. The upsides are obvious and extensive; not only does your partner not mind your company, other hikers are less likely to be repulsed by your 30-day post shower aroma.

Finally, physical affection on the trail, in tents or in town, requires a certain level of consideration. First and foremost is the issue of cleanliness: urinary tract infections are a real risk when both parties are as dirty as thru-hikers generally are, and these infections can range from moderately uncomfortable to pissing blood and needing a hospital visit. Though not a rule by any means, many romantic pairs remain purely platonic on trail and save the rest for hotels.

Not to mention that most sleeping pads are noisy enough with just one person on them!

• • •

I hope you are able to gain something from this bonus information for thru-hikers; if so, it would benefit us greatly if you could provide an honest review on this book's store page.

If you are a prospective thru-hiker yourself and want more information of any kind, please reach out to me. I will do my best to answer any questions or concerns. I would also love to hear about your thru-hike and post-trail experiences.

You can contact me by joining my Facebook author page at: https://www.facebook.com/CodyJamesHowellAuthor

Or by email at: RaidenATnineteen@gmail.com

ABOUT THE AUTHOR
Cody James Howell Phd, "Raiden"

Raiden is a successful Appalachian Trail thru-hiker and lifelong nature enthusiast. He has since been inducted into the "2000-miler club" for those who have walked the entire trail. Prior to hiking the AT, he completed a PhD in Neuroscience and published widely in academic journals. Now, he seeks to use these two distinct experiences to give back to the trail community. In 2021, Raiden will be traveling New Zealand with his wife Debra (Chilly Bin), a multi-trail thru-hiker he met on their second day hiking the Appalachian Trail. You can contact Raiden, and keep up with his ongoing projects, by following him on his Facebook author's page at Facebook.com/CodyJamesHowellAuthor or by emailing RaidenATnineteen@gmail.com.

Made in the USA
Coppell, TX
07 March 2021